wisdomsearches

wisdom
searches

Seeking

the

Feminine

Presence

of God

Nancy Chinn and Harriet Gleeson

Foreword by Elizabeth A. Johnson

THE PILGRIM PRESS   CLEVELAND, OHIO

The Pilgrim Press, Cleveland, Ohio 44115
© 1999 by Nancy Chinn and Harriet Gleeson

"Bless Sophia" by David Haas from *Bring the Feast: Songs from the Re-Imagining Community,* copyright © 1997 by The Pilgrim Press. Used by permission.

Biblical quotations in chapters 2, 5, 7, 8, and 9 are paraphrased from the New English Bible, © 1972 by Oxford University Press. Biblical quotations in chapters 3, 4, 6, and 10 are from the New Revised Standard Version of the Bible, © 1989 by the Division of Christian Education of the National Council of the Churches of Christ in the U.S.A.

Printed in Hong Kong on acid-free paper

04   03   02   01   00   99   5   4   3   2   1

Library of Congress Cataloging-in-Publication Data
Chinn, Nancy, 1940–
    Wisdom searches : seeking the feminine presence of God / Nancy Chinn and Harriet Gleeson ;
    foreword by Elizabeth A. Johnson.
        p.   cm.
    Includes bibliographical references.
    ISBN 0-8298-1338-1 (cloth : alk. paper)
    1. Femininity of God Prayer-books and devotions—English.   2. Wisdom (Biblical personification)
    Prayer-books and devotions—English.   I. Gleeson, Harriet, 1939–   II. Title.
    BT153.M6   C415   1999
    231'.4—dc21   99-32540
                                                                          CIP

Bless Sophia!

Dream the vision,

Share the wisdom

Dwelling deep within!

—David Haas, Prayer of the Re-Imagining Community, Minneapolis

Contents

*F*oreword

It is something of a wonder that as the third Christian millennium dawns, the symbolic figure of Wisdom is connecting so strongly with the experience of multitudes of women. When the history of spirituality of this age is written at some future date, authors will note the vigor with which women took Sophia into their hearts and lives, allowing her to open new pathways toward divine mystery and finding in her very femaleness a validation of their own sacred selves. No one in particular is orchestrating this rediscovery. Biblical texts and ancient prayers are uncovered, then passed around by word of mouth, by music, poetry, and painting, by shared rituals, or by discursive texts. As one flame enkindles another the light and warmth grow stronger, until whole groups of women experience together the power of her care. Not everyone is swept up by Wisdom, of course. But a growing cadre of women engaged in profoundly transforming life journeys nourish their hearts and souls at her table, to the point where it is unlikely that this symbol will disappear from memory anytime soon.

It was not always this way. For almost two thousand years the figure of Wisdom has rested in a very deep slumber, unremarked except for a slight relation to Christ sung in an Advent hymn ("O come, thou Wisdom, from on high") or uttered in a litany (Mary as Jesus' mother addressed as "Seat of Wisdom," meaning the throne on which Wisdom sits). It is interesting to note that in Catholic piety, Mary of Nazareth herself took on attributes of Wisdom, whose texts were read on Mary's feast days. But the powerful biblical scenes where Wisdom herself creates the world, redeems a people, cries out for justice, pours forth compassion, plays with the seasons, nourishes with her carefully prepared food, comforts and consoles, teaches the right path, sends forth heralds, utters her challenging word, renews all things, makes people friends of God and prophets, lights up evil and overcomes it—these extraordinary texts have played little or no role in people's spiritual life since they were written.

One reason seems to be that in scripture Wisdom operates outside, or at least independent of, law and covenant, priesthood and temple. Her teaching focuses not so much on once-for-all mighty divine acts in history, although these are remembered, but on "ordinary" time with its web of interpersonal and social relationships, seasonal changes, problems of conscience, and daily joys and sufferings. Unlike traditions of law and cult which were preserved and maintained by groups of elite males (Pharisees and Jerusalem priests, later rabbis), Wisdom escapes the control of any one group. Finding her center not in the temple but in the great world, she is given to anyone who searches out the order of creation in order to live in harmony with it. It is not, therefore, to the advantage of the religious ruling class to promote her ways.

One might think that in such a case those who are marginalized from most leadership positions, such as women in the first and second centuries before and after Christ, would find Wisdom their ally. But they did not, at least not in large enough numbers to be noticed. Perhaps one reason is that wisdom texts are embedded in longer treatises written with a strongly male-dominant point of view. Biblical Wisdom literature says some of the most hateful things about women on record. To liberate Wisdom from these texts, one needs a strong feminist hermeneutic that knows how to read between and behind the lines to reach the godly female figure imprisoned there. And this interpretive method cannot function at all unless it plays out as an expression of women's experience in all of its dimensions, many of which have traditionally been repressed but are now rising up in a great and powerful awakening.

This book is at once a sign that such a feminist interpretation is vigorously at the gates and a key that unlocks the potential held within. Written by two women on transformative life journeys, its chapters trace new categories of spirituality: right-relationship to the earth, care of the body, suffering through and out of suffering, risk-taking, relationships of heart and sexuality, anger, feasting. In every instance the left brain, so given to words, is enriched by the right brain and its power to summon up images. Together they chart a path along which these two women and Holy Wisdom rub up against each other, like silk that creates static or like flint that shoots off sparks. The friction ignites a fire that illuminates deep truths helpful to everyone else on the journey.

Now it becomes clearer than ever that people—women—connect with the holy mystery that surrounds their lives as they actually *live* in the world, in the "nonheroic" moments, in the effort to love and accept oneself, to be decent and just, in puzzling over past pain and present sufferings, in risking to reach out in love, in appreciating and caring for the earth and our bodies, in the gift and task of the everyday—in all this, every bit as much as in public religious ceremonies. Perhaps even more. And now it becomes clear that since Wisdom plays everywhere, the world cannot be neatly divided into sacred and profane times and places, any more than the divine mystery can be relegated to the transcendent realm to the neglect of her powerful indwelling. Even in its daily-ness, life mediates connections with the mystery of the Holy One, hidden and present.

Such is the vision of the biblical wisdom tradition, and such is the experience conveyed in this profoundly simple, beautifully drawn and written book. Read it and be encouraged. Meditate on it and be nourished into well-being.

ELIZABETH A. JOHNSON

Preface

This book offers sacred text, image, and reflection on both, for the consideration of the reader. The texts come from the sacred scriptures of the Hebrew and Christian traditions, the images and poems from one woman's immersion in what Wisdom/Sophia means to her. The narrative reflections are written from the context of a life lived in the Benedictine tradition of spirituality. The rule written by St. Benedict, founder of the monastic movement in the sixth century, slips into these discussions as easily and as effectively as the two-edged sword which is the Word of God. The rule of St. Benedict is in the tradition of Christian Wisdom literature, concerned as it is with the meaning and purpose of the lived (not thought about) life.

We invite you to listen with the "ear of your heart"[1] to both the images and the texts that inspired them, and to allow the images to move you to reflection on the place of Sophia in your life.

The subject matter here is sacred, concerned with our openness to the mysteries of the divine, our growth into unconditional acceptance of the Love that surrounds us. There is a deeply centered life abiding within each of us, a presence which despite our best efforts cannot in the end be ignored and which demands our attention. It is a presence and a life which will draw us into the Divine if we live with awareness.

This subject matter, then, needs to be approached in a manner suited to its great dignity. We, the authors, were ever mindful of this as we worked together doing the foundational writing for each chapter of this book.

Before each working session we established a beautiful space at our kitchen table, using candles, flowers, perhaps some earthy accompaniments of the kitchen, like salt or butter, and the image on which we were currently working. We invoked the presence and blessing of Sophia on our work and then read the relevant scripture passage aloud from two or more translations. For the next few minutes, in silence, we asked questions of the text and the image and listened for the response. We then wrote for a period of fifteen minutes without pause. At the end of this time we read our writings aloud to each other, exchanged some comment, and then returned to writing. At a time that seemed right we ceased writing and shared our writing out loud with each other. Then we closed with prayer to Sophia. After these sessions we worked separately to refine the work begun together.

The value of this method was twofold. First was the encouragement and support we afforded each other. This support made it easier to begin writing. Then, after starting, when inspiration sometimes seemed absent, the technique always prompted worthy reflection.

For the individual reader approaching the texts and the images, we suggest a method based on the Benedictine prayer practice of *lectio divina*. This relaxed, embodied method of prayerful reading is both simple and profound.

The context for the practice is a life spent seeking God, and the proper text for St. Benedict was the sacred scripture. The method, simple as it is, is underpinned by the profound belief, shared by all major religious and spiritual traditions, that prayerful reading and meditation on the sacred Word will lead to spiritual growth in the reader.

Often this assimilation of the divine Word is presented both in scripture and other church writings through images of eating and drinking.[2] The nature of *lectio* has been compared to chewing the cud, a remarkably earthy image. Ruminating on a word or phrase, repeatedly bringing it up for prayerful consideration, allows us to eat deliberately, deeply, and richly of the divine food as we open ourselves to layers and depths of meaning.

The practice is simple. Before beginning, prepare a place conducive to meditative reading. Perhaps have a centering candle to recall your attention if it wanders, collect yourself in the presence of the Divine and begin to murmur the text aloud. When a word or phrase stands out for you, repeat it over and over and be conscious of the prayer that rises in your heart. When the prayer is over, return to the text and begin again to murmur. The gifts of this kind of prayer can be many: perhaps the fact that we have prayed is enough, perhaps insight, perhaps a most precious gift—the experience of a moment of contemplation.

So proceed in awareness and find the simplicity and profundity that are characteristics of the journey to the Sacred Center. Seek with your mind and with your heart, and your soul will unfold.

> There is no safety, and there is no end.
> The word must be heard in silence;
> there must be darkness to see the stars.
> The dance is always danced above the hollow place, above the terrible abyss.[3]

1

Our Biographies

Nancy Chinn's Story

I tell you my story to suggest only one truth: if you are reading this, you are part of a community of women and men, all sorts of men and women, who are on a deep and lengthy journey to find God.

Such a journey has many paths.

Some of you began from my own tradition of Christianity, but others are finding your way through Hinduism, or tribal religions, or Jewish traditions, or Buddhist, Wiccan, Islamic, or any of a multitude of religious traditions that led you to this place in your journey. Most of us have discovered that an arduous pilgrimage gives us times of reluctantly casting away what was once quite familiar and comforting.

This is because our lives had shown us other realities, other inconsistencies, and other truths. We simply could no longer accept what we had been taught, and we could find no room at our old altars for who we have become. Perhaps with grief, perhaps with relief, or fear, curiosity or wonder, we have turned aside from our old cultures and ways of worship. For me, part of the difficulty was to set aside a vast and demanding family of my tradition, the community of worshipers that had sustained me through most of my life. I felt as though I was alone on this journey. That aloneness felt full of pain and shame, yet I knew from my dreams and from reflection on my life that there was no other way I could live. I understood my life was now to be that of the exile.

Perhaps that is how it was for you too.

As this book is being written, your faces flash before us. Though you are unknown to us by name, we know you as companions in a common quest. Pilgrims, seeking out a truth not yet clear to us, we offer you our stories, not as markers along the way but as hands to join as we traverse this path of the heart. Come, hear about her, the one hidden within the traditions of Christianity and Jewish thinking. Let her way of being challenge the assumptions and privileges of religious ideology. Watch her truth emerge from where she has been buried, and listen to her comfort and her promises. These revelations are meant for you and for all who seek the feminine face of God.

My own journey is clearest if I look backwards. It is upon reflection that I see the patterns and can find the shape of the map I am following. The long arms of a spiral mark its form, as I visit and revisit time and space with one theme: Who is God and how am I, a woman, made in this image?

My own family life of origin was quite broken. Somehow, moving at least once every year to a new community, I discovered that I could find a home and acceptance within a local church. This became a constant in my life. We would move, and I would find a church to attend by myself, and immerse myself in all it could offer a poor and rootless wanderer. Even then, my questioning mind would challenge: where are the women? How is God a father and not a mother? If we are to become the brotherhood of men, how do I do that and remain female? How I longed to have that male privilege! Looking back on those times, I know that if I had been male, my teachers and mentors would have encouraged me toward theological study. Yet, this was the late 1940s, women were not permitted significant leadership within the academic and ecclesiastical communities, and I was often ignored or told to act more like a woman and not to challenge what was being taught. How many of us had our minds so channeled by well-intentioned but misguided leadership?

Yet the church welcomed me with large, open arms, and finding little in my home that spoke of love, I walked willingly into this doctrine, hoping that I could somehow quiet the questions and still the raging doubts. I had many experiences of God, many times when I knew this Holy Presence through inner voice, my dreams, and flashes of deep knowing. Fervently I sang, prayed, and read, seeking my place in this huge cosmic plan. I entered junior high, senior high, and finally college and marriage . . . to a seminary student.

Somewhere during that time I became aware that Catholics and Protestants had different Bibles. Why? I asked, and then I was told that in some Catholic books God was seen as a woman, and that is not right, is it? No, I shook my head, but not my heart. Vowing to find out the reason for this divergence in holy text, I learned New Testament Greek and translated enough of the Bible myself to perceive the cultural bias of language and realize that the translators had as much to do with the content as the words themselves. We lose much subtlety moving between our languages.

It was with the birth of my daughter, Robin, and my sons, Stephen and Jason, that the rise of feminist consciousness blew across my own life. Week by week, as I read voraciously all the early feminist literature of the early 1970s, I found the high walls of patriarchal thinking that enclosed every corner of my life being dismantled. Inequalities between men and women in the political arena, in the workplace, in academia and the church showed me the misogynist thinking in our culture. But it was in my personal life, where I was more function than person within my marriage, that my rebellion became most clarion. I could no longer accept an assigned place within the establishment.

I was among the lucky. An invitation to join with other women of all traditions who were seeking a new path came across my desk. Can you imagine the fierceness in my whole body when I said yes to this opportunity? Together we stumbled monthly to try to represent our traditional festivals and holidays as they might be if women's experiences were the source of ritual. Together with Jews, Protestants, Catholics, Buddhists, Muslims, and Wiccans we rolled around the calendar celebrating a banquet of different traditions, using fresh and imaginative ways to celebrate those events. All of us understood that God is more than gender. But it was important to counter the phallocentric theology of our traditions—as one person put it, "for health." We also understood that to undo the knowledge we had learned through ritual, we had to learn new ways through praxis, not as an intellectual activity.

During this time, my spouse came home from teaching Hebrew one day to announce to me that they had been working on Genesis, and he wanted me to know that the Spirit hovering above the deep unformed was *feminine* in the Hebrew! Astounded, I plunged in, and with my tools as an artist, I explored the Genesis story through my own painting process. First through acrylics, then watercolor, then murals, and finally papercuts, I created four series based on this story. I began to understand how this story had been misused to blame women for original sin.

During this time also, I began to struggle with the visual elements of traditional Protestant worship. What we proclaimed in word, reading, and song and what we proclaimed visually just did not match. I began making art for proclamation, and quite quickly began making it with interested members of my congregation. The scale of the art and its placement alone demanded attention. The planning necessary to make the artwork appropriately integrate with the themes of worship began to alter the impact of the services. To date, the number of installations of this architecturally scaled art (huge) far exceeds five hundred, and it has been shown in most denominations here and abroad.

What I have found is that this art process interrupts the hierarchical presumptions about the content of worship. As a result, the experience of worship becomes far more holistic and integrated. The work itself was often made from materials traditionally considered feminine: fabric, ribbon, pattern, lace, and ephemeral materials. Unlike normal art, this was not a product to be bought and sold. Usually it was site- and event-specific. Secretly, I knew it was a subversive act to make this art, and it was a way to integrate my feminist thinking within my tradition.

Meanwhile my own personal painting began to take a new direction as I created with a highly erotic abstract quality. I abandoned landscapes and portraiture to follow the intuitive, and highly feminine, forms that I watched come forth from my brush and paints. As I worked, I began to know my deeper self.

Abruptly my marriage of twenty-four years ended. Feeling suicidal, with my God, my home, and my life in turmoil, I began an exile. Somehow, day by day, year by year, with my art making as my only root, I moved through this sad and dangerous chapter of my life.

During this time, I began to look at the Goddess. At first these were just tiny glimpses, and I would return to my own religious roots, chafing there with the language that spoke only of male realities. Uncomfortable with her because of all the years of shunning by the church, theaphobic at my core, I could not face her for long. Turning away, I would yet find her again, gazing upon me, waiting for me at every corner. Finally in desperation I jumped off, returned her gaze, and floated into her presence.

To my shock, there was a new community: my artist sisters and brothers who had gone before me and could show me new ideas, new ways of seeing God in this feminine form. My spirituality moved beyond the old voices of the church, and beyond definition. My questions began to find answers, not just intellectual ones, but answers of resonance through my entire being. I began to hear God again, the voice I had once heard as a child. The spiral of my life had begun to return to its origin again.

Yet I am Christian by culture. My feet remain planted in this orientation. I still make art about it. After reading Phyllis Tribble's *Texts of Terror,* I created a series of ten (a minyan) stories of women from the Bible who were abused by the tradition and whose abuse continues even in today's culture. This work was shown in countless churches.

But it was the community of Re-Imagining that brought me home. Originally organized as a conference of feminist theologians in Minneapolis, Minnesota, in

November 1993, and largely ignored by everyone except conservative denominational presses, it grew into an ongoing, independently funded organization. Privileged to be involved in planning and leading the community in art making during the first conference, for the first time I found out that my story was part of a much larger surge of stories, and I was not alone any longer! Ecstatic, I found freshness and renewal in the call of Sophia, with links to both biblical tradition and feminine experience.

Deeply disturbed by the negative reaction to this conference, I began reading carefully about Sophia, finding Elizabeth Johnson's work *She Who Is* especially helpful. I was intrigued to learn that all biblical references to Wisdom are always feminine, never neuter, never masculine. Then came a call from Re-Imagining: could I paint something about Sophia that could be a poster for a fund-raiser? Returning to Johnson's texts, I began what is the series of paintings in this book. Sometimes I painted reflecting on the text. Other times I began paintings, and then found the texts appropriate to clarify the paintings as they became complete.

All the paintings are intuitive. I began with a stroke, a gesture, and then built upon that with color, form, and, at times, collage, in watercolor and waterbased mixed media.[1] I did not plan them or do sketches for them. Reflection on the texts, prayer, and a relational attitude toward my painting has been the guiding path. I consider these icons. My prayer is that you will find the paintings and writings doorways to your own creative responses, and that you also will discover Sophia's presence emerge from beneath the layers and dusts of time as you do your work.

Harriet Gleeson's Story

I have had a number of lives. I was born in countrified suburban Brisbane, an Australian city scorned by the sophisticated southerners as slow, humid, and out of the loop of culture and interest.

I walked and played in eucalyptus bush and steamy heat, wearing few, light clothes. I remember being covered with orange mango juice from my face to my feet. Painstakingly peeling the skin from "quarters" of mandarins growing next door in Granny's yard. Walking on fences, building mud dams, and floating boats in rainy weather. Sitting in the sand "under the house" and watching ant lions catch and eat their prey. Building miniature gardens in tins. Going to my uncle's farm for the holidays, boys' and girls' teams competing to see who could eat the most passion fruit; eating honey from the comb and fresh peanuts, just dug.

It was in some ways a good childhood, but there was a pervading cloud of anxiety throughout these and my teenage years. I lived with the constant shadow of my mother erupting in insane and apparently unprovoked rage. I believe she was ill, but in those days one did not own to mental illness, which was considered a disgrace. My strategy was to read, and read, and read, living in worlds and bodies that were not my own, as often and as long as possible. The holidays at the farm with my cousins, which I dearly enjoyed, stopped too, when my mother and my aunt quarreled. I became a teenage misfit and struggled painfully to conceal my misfitness from my mother. During all this time I experienced a love of God and an interest in religion. I went to Mass more often than required, attended Benediction of the Blessed Sacrament, joined the Children of Mary sodality, walked in May processions and Corpus Christi processions, and somehow came to see that I would be a nun. One day at our Catholic primary school, the Mother Superior of the teaching nuns came to see the school. She asked our class who was going to be a nun. All the girls in the class put up their hands except me. I knew they were not intending that profession, and putting up their hands offended my sense of propriety.

At twenty-one years of age I entered the convent, no doubt for many reasons but certainly for the love of God, and I remained there over thirty years. These years were important for me in many ways. The early years prior to Vatican II were difficult. After Vatican II the congregation renewed itself by recovering its Benedictine roots. The Benedictine tradition in which I was formed is solid, commonsensical, and deeply spiritual. In that tradition the daily recitation of the psalms is a key element of life, and one which I find deeply satisfying to this day. Many of the women with whom I lived were wonderful models of womanhood. I prayed the prayers of the church without much consciousness of their masculine language and bias, though I do remember getting a little upset once when the words of a prayer for women martyrs went something like "O God, we give you thanks that *even* weak women . . . " I had good moments in prayer. My image of God was definitely masculine for many years, and then, I think, it got very spiritual so that I could ignore the masculine bits and pieces. Eventually I began to find some indications that to think of God in female terms was appropriate for me.

After thirty years in the convent I was given the wonderful gift of time, free of responsibilities, to renew my life. I enrolled in a program engineered for the task of renewal, having made two promises in prayer: that I would work as far as possible in art and symbol, and that I would do anything required of me by God. The second promise was powerful! The entry to the path was laid out for me very clearly, and extraordinary things began to happen. Synchronicity came into play and almost anything I read or saw or did linked into the task of the moment.

I became aware of an interest in the Goddess rising in me. I had not done any specific work on the topic and I had read no books about it. I think the atmosphere of the place where I did the renewal was permeated with thoughts and energies of the Feminine Divine. I am now a little amused at my first reaction to my awareness, which was to be appalled—worship of the Goddess was pagan and I could not be involved in it! But as I continued to work on my spiritual journey, reaction to the masculinity of the church and of life in general began to disturb me. Becoming convinced of the truth of the statement that we can only speak in metaphors about God, I began to look for feminine metaphors which would be helpful to me. Of course, I found Sophia, who in the Catholic tradition has been conflated with Christ. This is fine with me, for Julian calls Christ "Mother," and it all goes around in a circle.

At the end of those life-giving and liberating two years, I made a life-changing decision. Prior to this time I would not have been able to make a decision of this magnitude about my own life. But now, with the aid of Sophia, I left my life as a nun to live in a one-to-one relationship. The decision was wise, as the relationship calls me to different, and for me harder, work than did my life in the convent.

While this life relationship is my lifework now, I do not feel complete in my journey. I am discovering more aspects of myself daily and revisiting many old ones, if at a different level each time. I am also understanding more of Sophia's guidance as I continue to grow. It is my hope that as you read of my journey your own particular path to God will come more clearly into focus for you. Blessings.

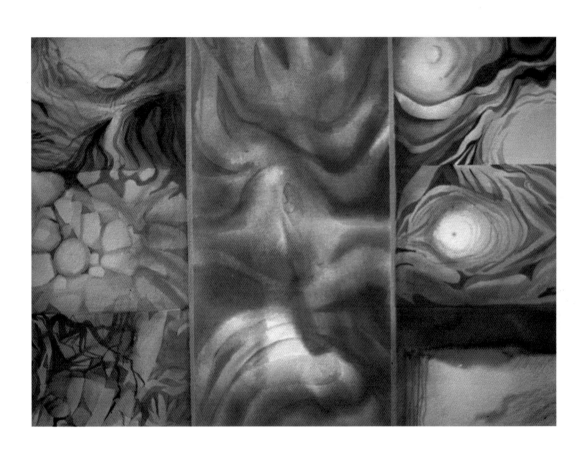

2

Wisdom Teaches

God gave me true understanding of things as they are:

a knowledge of the structure of the world

and the operation of the elements;

the beginning and the end of epochs

and their middle course;

the alternating solstices and changing seasons;

the cycles of the years and the constellations;

the nature of living creatures and the behavior of wild beasts;

the violent force of winds and the thoughts of humans;

the varieties of plants and the virtues of roots.

I learned it all, hidden or manifest,

for I was taught by her whose skill made all things, Wisdom.

—WISDOM 7:17–22

SONG LINE

Chaos greets me daily.
    I clean it, sort it,
     toss and store away.
But it rises again with the next dawn,
yeasty, smelling like infection.

You know a place beneath such turmoil.
    You have wound it tightly
     into categories, systems, cycles.
You arranged all decently and in order.
The map lies buried to this treasure.

You plaited the patterns of storms,
    the scream of cats piercing night's thickness;
     the torque of root boring earth
from wind-tossed acorns lying still on paths.
Your hand craftings leave long memories.

Overwhelmed again, I toss up my will,
    bogged in moods that rage their violent storms.
     Quiet teacher, sing through my stumbling ways.
Sharpen my ear, my eye, my heart,
that I might hum the harmony holding all.

Searchings

Lady Wisdom, Teacher, you were there at the creation. Wisdom who illuminates, Wisdom who is much more than facts, you know the essence and the purpose of all things. Help me to know the purpose of all around me, of nature, of people, of things. Help me to truly know my place within creation.

For some time now I have felt a growing yearning to enter into friendship with the rest of creation, to understand my place in it and its place in the providence of God. I long to really know the mysteries of which, from time to time, I get a fleeting glimpse of understanding.

I long to break out of the attitudes to nature in which I have been formed by my upbringing. For many centuries the Christian churches and our society have educated us in the developed world to exist separate from our bodies and to venerate the mind and its power above the rest of us or, (perish the thought) the whole of us. I am struck by the irony of using the word "developed" in this context.

On the contrary, most native peoples of this earth possessed the great gift of living in harmony with nature, of understanding nature's epiphanic relationship to the Divine. Life for them was seamless. They did not live with compartments of sacred and secular. I give thanks that all of their teaching and lifestyle have not disappeared. We still have a chance to learn from their Wisdom. Lady Wisdom is moving strongly now, for I, like many women and men these days, have come to a place where I feel an urgent and instinctive need to make connections with creation, to come into right relationship with it.

In general our Western relationship with creation to date has been a power struggle. We have so far mastered many aspects of nature or, at least, we think we have. Our physics has allowed us to develop machinery and industry and has taken us to the moon. We have harnessed water for power and irrigation. We have discovered and used the power of the atom. Now, however, we are beginning to understand that we have not in fact mastered nature. We have manipulated aspects of nature only to find that we are destroying this earth on which we live. Consequences of our cavalier attitude toward nature are being seen in the oceans, the atmosphere, and organisms including humankind.

A gift from my bread-and-butter activity of teaching geometry has been my discovery of the math of fractals. There is much that the metaphor of fractals has to tell me, and I am straining to pick it up. What I have now with fractals is a tool for understanding nature in a different way.

The complex and beautiful image which is a fractal is the pictorial result of plotting what happens when a very simple mathematical equation is repeated over and over again with the answer from each calculation used as the input for the next iteration. In other words, simple causes can lead to complex results. This is something we all instinctively know, I think—but the earlier mathematicians couldn't find it.

These fractal images have intricate edges, beautiful shapes, and astounding properties. Fractals (mathematical models) are self-replicating at different dimensions—that is, if we look at the whole and then look at a small part of the whole we will see the whole shape again in miniature.

An example of fractal nature is the cauliflower. Looking at the whole cauliflower we see trunk and branches. Remove a branch and look at it alone, and see again the original pattern of trunk and branches. If we put this small piece under a magnifying glass we would see the original cauliflower shape. And if we removed a smaller branch from the small piece and magnified it, what would we see? Of course, the whole cauliflower.

For another example, if we look at the coastline of Australia, we notice the roughness of bays and headlands. If we select just a small length of coastline and magnify it, we see again the roughness of bays and headland. We could continue this process indefinitely if we had powerful enough magnifying glasses, and the smallest length of land we could see would still look like the larger coastline. So when we zoom in on the coastline we see smaller and smaller self-replications of the general shape. Surprisingly, we find it is impossible to measure the true length of the coastline of Australia because however careful we are, we can never measure the length of all the infinitesimal bays and headlands.

My students drew fractals. Given a basic straight-line shape, they squeezed the whole shape onto each straight-line section of the original, so we had the pattern repeated many times and much smaller. At the next repeat the whole pattern was squeezed again and drawn on each straight-line segment of the previous pattern, and so on until the pencil was too thick to trace any more paths. What is happening here? The pencil path at each repeat is longer and the area being covered by graphite is decreasing for each repetition of the path. So we have infinite length bounding limited area—something to turn our thought patterns upside-down! And note: all the activity is at the edge.

This seems to suggest also that rough edges define the beauty and organization of nature. The picture of nature we now have is of layers of complexity alternating with layers of simplicity. We see the mystery of infinite length surrounding limited area. We know that small changes in prevailing conditions lead to enormous changes in outcome, we see the infinitely growing convoluted edges.

My math-teaching compatriots and I were on the computer, zooming in on (magnifying) a set of fractal images called the Mandelbrot set (named "The Thumbprint of God"). Starting with the shape of the whole image we selected one tiny fringe on the edge of the image and magnified it. We then focused on a tiny portion of that magnified image and repeated the process over and over, looking at smaller and smaller portions of the original. We continued to zoom down and down. Each time we zoomed we saw startling and beautiful images.

After maybe twenty zooms we could only gasp with amazement as we saw, in the middle of one minute part of the original image, tiny and perfect in its entirety, the complete image of the Mandelbrot set with which we had begun. The astonishing thing is that if our computer had the power we could zoom through the same series of images and again find another image, infinitely smaller, of the whole. As one of my students said with awe, "Fractals never end."

Fractal study of nature reveals that underlying any complex situation is a layer of organization. When something, even something very small, happens to disrupt the system it is thrown into chaos (complexity) until it reaches a new stable state and a new underlying pattern of organization. We perceive that in nature simplicity underlies complexity, underlies simplicity, to infinity.

I am reminded as I work with fractals of the end of *The Last Battle* by C. S. Lewis. The children and creatures are racing exultantly and impossibly up mountains and waterfalls, following the call of "Further up and further in!" Eventually they pause and Lucy, leaning on the garden wall, looks out and down to where they have come from. As the land below comes into focus, she sees that there are many Narnias, each nestled inside the last, and that their journey has taken them in and in and in again to the center. Not only is their beloved country of Narnia safe but it is becoming more and more real, more and more beautiful at each repeat and larger and larger as they move to the next inner circle. As the faun Tumnus says, "The inside is larger than the outside."

Mandelbrot claims that the human brain is fractal and that we have been deprived of the richness of this part of ourselves because math and science had no way of coping with the perceived complexity of nature and consequently simplified our math and physics. Mathematical models had the difficulties smoothed out, along with our perceptions, so that the math of the time could handle them. With the advent of computers and the discovery of the math of fractals, we begin to appreciate and deal with the complexity of nature. Now we all, mathematicians, artists, theologians, humankind, are able to reclaim our perceptions as accurate, to see the mystery in nature which harmonizes with our own created being. Now our learned perceptions are being turned downside-up!

In the painting with this chapter, I find many aspects of the creation. In the middle, I find a shape moving, almost dancing between the smaller shapes on the sides. The outer aspects do not remain enclosed, but move between each other, connecting with each other. Yet the center remains enclosed, in and yet not of creation.

Lady Wisdom, bring me gifts of perception and faithfulness; bring me into right relation with creation; keep me on the path to right relationship with myself. Join me as I revel in mystery.

WAYS OF KNOWING

Faith

Some faith I learned in Sunday school.
I've read and heard, with hungry ears.
I watched, spine chilled, as Heston split the sea,
I've sung and prayed and testified,
felt the presence, heard the voice.
But this faith could not, would not,
did not sustain my broken heart.
Now faith I trust is truth that rises
still as the place where darkness yields to day.
I mine within to find my words,
buried deep, for I am old.
Faith pours from cells and ancient bones,
treasure, just uncovered,
savored slowly, a rare fine wine.

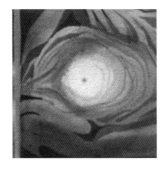

Hope

It first arrived with Santa Claus,
then found its way to dances, and growing woman-signs;
sweet hopes, yet small, as greater hopes arose;
my marriage, and the birth of three,
for a world where they could grow
and thrive. How little did I know!
My hopes grew small and dim again,
battered feathers, cast aside.
Expect a future, lose a now.
Beneath thin hope lies greater vision.
It takes long eyes to discern this sight,
and a heart as empty as the sea.

Love

And love, proud love, where did you go?
I learned of you in children's tales,
those happy-ever-afters
where weddings are the happiest days.
Why did I weep so long at mine?
Love meant passion, strife, and struggle,
childhood wounds, disguised as wisdom.
Now I know of love transformed
as barren trees in winter's dreams,
whose long, strong limbs and branches link
mirroring roots, anchored deep below. So love!
Roots that spring from self-respect grow canopies
where love abides in mutuality,
the strongest, most enduring of the three.

3

Wisdom Rises

For Wisdom is more mobile than any motion;

because of her pureness she pervades and

   penetrates all things.

For she is a breath of the power of God,

and a pure emanation of the glory of the Almighty.

—WISDOM 7:24–25A

ZIMZUM

Sometimes the weight of life
    squeezes like birth
    forcing us forward
        wailing
    for what has been lost
    and what we must endure.

Sobbing screams, or soundless grief,
    heart-bending labors
    to earn our daily
        breads,
    and still we strive,
    still cling to life and breath.

Other times are born,
    smelling of moist breath,
    tugging desires,
        promising
    sweet tastes,
    love just begun.

God blew across primordial mud,
    and Adam gasped first breath.
    Often Jesus blew
        Spirit.
    Old bones grasped strength
    to learn to walk another way.

Suck and surge of water's edge,
    breathing land, blowing sea,
    life's lines ever turn,
        spinning.
    Tasks rise like mountains,
    Gifts fall as rain.

Pilgrim, you travel,
> not to place
> but for the journey
> > alone.
> Savor your dryness.
> Seize space for joy.[1]

Space for Symbols

Sophia, your image here is spiraling in to the home place, out to mystery. Edges firm yet soft, place of luminous dark and hospitable light. You are the path. We journey into you, with you; journey into ourselves, with you. We cannot in the end get lost. "This is the place where the longed-for will happen, This is the time when the longed-for will come. . . . Set your feet to the path, for there is no other way."[2] I have walked this spiral path now for many years, I recognize the spiral, I recognize that as we spiral in, our life, our knowing expands. Contemplating the portion of my life journey of the last five or six years, I celebrate some features of the path over which you have led me.

Throughout my early adult life I was always seduced by symbol. I recognized in symbol a power of connection with people, places, and events, which I longed to own. I was envious of the friends I observed assembling items which carried important memory for them on their altars or tables or walls, and was conscious that I was missing something significant.

Many is the time I followed a retreat leader's instructions to "find something in the garden which represents part of you. . . ." Always I dutifully found a dry twig representing my dryness, or a slightly budding twig signifying my death/resurrection. In these exercises there was always a sense of contrivance; none of these symbols ever connected deeply and truly with my experiences.

I also made very deliberate efforts to assemble personal symbols, tried to attach meaning and memory of places, and so on, but it did not work: I never felt connection with the symbol. It makes sense to me now as I reflect on my life at that time when I was keeping parts of my life and personality split off from other parts. My relationships were unsatisfactory through my own ineptitude. The truth was that I was homeless in every sense. The absence of symbol was the truth of my state over all those years.

At age fifty I was given a remarkable gift by my religious congregation of significant time off from my normal working life to pause and take stock, to reflect on my life so far.

This precious time was spent in the context of a place, personnel, and structure designed to support this renewal activity. I am conscious of the privilege I received, not available to many people, of time available without anxiety about life's necessities.

What the gift of untrammeled time allowed me was to work deliberately and consciously with my inner agenda. Two important decisions came to me as I prepared to move to this place and time of transition: after thirty-odd years of living and working out of my head, of following rules and dogma imposed on me, of being constantly fearful, I recognized a power and a yearning inside myself to work in symbol and art. I also said, "I will be open to everything that happens."

When I gave myself to the process, the symbols of my renewal journey arrived in their own time and as powerful gifts. The symbols included images in artwork; dreams and twilight images; the body with its sensations and feelings; poetry; natural objects and human artifacts. They arrived with a clarity and intensity that could not allow misinterpretation: they carried my truth.

The symbols not only carried my personal truth, but were connections with the collective unconscious. I was profoundly astonished when I first became aware of this. Now I am left with feelings of awe as I realize that I have been equipped to enter the mysterious and illimitable ocean of human and specifically women's experience.

Just before coming to the renewal program in Berkeley, I began the imaging process which has been so powerful throughout this portion of my journey. The beginning was not pleasant: I recognized with loathing and fear an image inside myself: a tunnel extending down through the center of my body, dark, soft, and wet with the softness of decay, repulsive, admitting no light and allowing no self-appreciation.

This image of tunnel was an important one. The experiences of tunnel in fact provided me with a powerful integrative tool for healing. After embarking on my renewal program I began to experience frightening dreams and twilight images involving tunnels. These presented a variety of situations. In some I was fighting my way through tunnels which were too narrow or blocked, in others I was falling out of control into tunnels.

These experiences occurred throughout the whole of the first nine months (it was two academic semesters of my renewal: I have just realized that it is the gestation period!). In December I went to Carmel for some quiet retreat days. On the night of the 14th of December I had another twilight image experience:

To Carmel. Good to be here . . . Tired . . . Twilight image of walking off the shelf into the trench in the ocean. Very frightening. Then I attempted to go down deliberately to try to make friends with this bogy. Found myself once again traveling through a tunnel—dark and light. Nothing came of it.

Two days later, while sightseeing around Carmel, I had to pass through a tunnel under the highway in order to reach a cliffside waterfall. I walked down a slope unsuspecting, came around a corner, and was face to face with a tunnel about twenty yards in front of me. I walked toward it, still unsuspecting. When I reached the mouth of the tunnel, suddenly I was not able to walk on through it. My legs gave way, my stomach heaved, and my head became dazed. I stood for some seconds unable to move.

In Julia Pfieffer Park . . . the tunnel. It was a disturbing experience. I thought that I would not be able to walk through it. Muscles and intestines went to water. All rational control in my head cut out involuntarily.

Eventually I remembered the person accompanying me who was some way behind me. She was not one to engage with symbol, and the thought of explaining or of not being able to explain was too much for me. I breathed deeply and forced myself to walk into the mouth of the tunnel.

The first steps into the mouth of the tunnel were difficult, but I did walk in and through, wondering all the time while I was on the other side what was going to happen on the way back. In fact the experience did not recur on the return walk through the tunnel.

One day during this time I was presented with the opportunity of building and then walking a labyrinth. Thus I discovered a symbol to encompass my life journey. The beautiful symmetry of the copy of the labyrinth in Chartres Cathedral invites my eye and my heart. I am intrigued and feel a sense of mystery every time I see the pattern of the labyrinth bending back and forth, approaching the mysterious center. Crossing the threshold is a solemn business with a feeling of commitment to whatever might develop, so I remove my shoes and pause for a while. Walking the labyrinth, I am anxious to arrive at the center. Eventually I see only one barrier between me and the center and I believe I am almost there, but after the next turn I find that I am as far from the center as I can possibly be. Sometimes I walk with my back to the center, losing sight of it. Sometimes I face the center open-eyed.

So I learned many things: that the path, the journey, is the element with which I must spend the most time; though I am not always focused on the journey I can return and find myself on the path. I persevere on the path, and eventually, and unexpectedly, I am at the center. I have come to understand that the center of the labyrinth carries the meanings of all the centers to which I journey in my life: Sophia and my deepest self. I remain in the center but know I cannot stay there indefinitely. I need to journey out again, carrying a gift of some new clarity or new inspiration, to bring to my life of every day. On my journey, if I am not alone in the labyrinth, I need to adjust my pace to others also walking, or I need to pause or pass. My journey is not mine alone. The journey is rhythmic, to the center and back. It reminds me of the importance of rhythm in my life.

Symbol was the powerful tool that united all elements of the journey. It moved my journey more powerfully and quickly than I thought possible. It expressed my passion, needs, hopes, and fears and the state of my spirit and relationship with Goddess to a degree which gave me intense satisfaction. It expressed profoundly the mystery and fullness of promise available to me if I persevered in the journey.

Sophia, you are the path on which I walk, the labyrinth of my life. Let me walk in gratitude for the love and strength and beauty of the journey so far. Let me walk in perseverance to meet the difficulties I will encounter. Let me listen deeply with the ear of my heart, always spiraling, coming home again and again, at each turn knowing more deeply where is my home, where is my center.

TURNING

One

It has rained many days.
Our sun lies low, unremembered.
My skin sours with downpours,
my spirit strains for deserts.

or

Parched, the earth so dry
my garden hose alone
cannot pierce the crusted soil.
Drought burns all seeds of hope or bloom.

Two

Scorned, I boil in self-absorption.
Rage simmers anger with pity
into a stew of revenge-filled
retribution.

or

Basking with honors for life well-lived,
benevolent, I pass spare-change signs,
pressing coins to the hands of all who reach.
I am a queen bestowing tiny mercies.

Three

I am bone weary,
the bed cannot absorb my fatigue.
Turning about, covers rising and falling,
tossing pillows, I search for sleep.

or

Also curious, even in the dark,
bored with bed, I rush to paint.
My nightclothes grow stars,
stains of mauves and blues.

Yet Again

I deserve constancy! Life must not change!
Enduring endless suffering, or grasping scraps of heaven,
I confuse the destination with the path. Bewildered,
I zig and zag between the fullness and the voids.

and

You stretch there too, like liquid love,
pouring patiently past these patterns,
coaxing my spirit to understand,
beckoning me to walk my path again.

4

In Her Hand

Long life is in her right hand;

in her left hand are riches and honor.

—PROVERBS 3:16

O ANTIPHONS

Sky Sweeper, brushing dust from stars,
    cast your shimmering tent of green,
    enfolding nests and ripening fruits,
    clinging to thick and shifting earths.
    Bridging centuries lived day by day,
O Tree of Life,
    feed me 'til I want no more.

Sowing the Word like wind-tossed seeds
    of Wisdom, borne in hearts and memories,
    you root me in my people.
    Torah, Koran, Gospel, myth and tale,
    Bread of Heaven, Well, or Salt,
O Word of God,
    fill me 'til I want no more.

Map of Meaning, Dawning Love,
    soft, sweet stirrings of secret places,
    quiet darkness, dream-tossed nights;
    and then your touch, and smile, and voice,
    your kiss and open heart: beloved gifts!
O Hand, O Heart, O Breath of God,
    find me 'til I'm lost no more!

Enchanter of Commonplace, romance my senses
    with tangs of tangelo, the comforts of quilts,
    fleeting fragrance from front-path freesias,
    the heart-gasping glory of storm-broken sunsets,
    or mockingbirds' trills to crisp morning stars!
O Lavish Lover, O Glorious Grace,
    touch me, 'til I am no more!

Worries and Fears

In your right hand is length of days; in your left hand is wealth and honor. Lady Wisdom, as I read the text and meditate on the painting in this chapter, what rises for me are two things: dealing with difficult memories (a current worry), and dealing with fear (a lifetime task).

Reading Rumi last night I was given a gift that is important to me right now. Rumi exhorts us to welcome all the dark visitors, including shame and fear, to the guest house which is our self. In this welcoming, he says, we will be healed.

I have recently been urgently aware of the need to deal with the shadows of past failure in my life. Some old ghosts are popping up, completely unannounced, at any time of the day or night, overwhelming me with feelings of incompetence and shame. I cannot believe how stupid or inept I was. These experiences are not comfortable, but I recognize that my psyche is again coming to my aid!

After some false starts, mostly trying to suppress the experiences and then deal with them rationally, I am being taught, perforce, that I must look at them squarely. More than that, I am being taught to welcome them, to throw my arms open to them, in order to allow them to release growth and love into my life. This I recognize as truth on the rational level. After all, this insight has been presented to me before—many times. The spiritual and psychological teachers all say it. Now, though, I am struggling to understand it in my body. Now, sometimes torn and shamed inside, I am beginning to come to this round of healing. I have come round the spiral again.

While reading the poem of Rumi that prompted me into prayerful reflection on this part of my life, I was reminded of St. Benedict: "All guests who present themselves are welcomed as Christ. . . . He is indeed welcomed in them." So, not only will I ask Christ to welcome these guests with me, but astonishingly, I am also welcoming Christ in them. This is a profound and extraordinary discovery!

My Lenten journey this year was to work with Christ with these experiences. One of the profound gifts to me this Easter was reinforcement of this purpose by a remark from a chance-met acquaintance. I forgot the remark almost as soon as I heard it, but not what it triggered. This was a startlingly clear invitation/instruction from my deepest self, to invite Christ to be with me in greeting these unwelcome guests.

As soon as I reached home and quietness I ritualized this grace, and formally asked Christ to accompany me in welcoming and loving these spurned selves. Since this time I ask Christ to be with me whenever one of these uninvited guests turns up. I feel a most comforting and loving presence and I can begin to love those selves of mine which I have long ignored. Continued blessing follows. I have experienced Christ in my body. I have experienced presence, and warmth, and security.

The Easter homily slipped into this scenario with ease and grace: The disciples, seeing that Jesus was ready to take the rap, fled. When they subsequently found the tomb open and empty, they would not have been happy! They would have asked: What will happen now? What will he say to us? What will he do? "We do not celebrate new life," said the homilist; "that doesn't always ring true. What we celebrate is the attitude of the risen Christ, who did not scold or blame but who brought forgiveness and reconciliation." Christ and I do welcome the ghosts of the past!

Such guides and companions as I describe as my experience of Christ belong particularly to one tradition. Yet I know little of others' traditions. My curiosity to know of other guides in other faiths rises. Might I know their companionship also? Could these various guides and companions indeed all be from the same source, just called by different names?

Yet I cannot help returning to reflect on the rich sequence of blessings, directions, hints, and helps which came together over a short period of time while I began to deal with the issue of my ghosts. I have noticed time and time again in my life that if I am aware of an issue to be dealt with, and if I have a will to deal with it, I am lavished with blessing. Our God is a generous God.

Which brings me back to the painting, to the munificent hands of Lady Wisdom holding life, wealth, and honor. I see them also as a tree of life and I am moved

to climb the tree

to embrace it

to eat of its fruit

to feel canopied by its foliage

to fold myself in the hands of the divine.

The painting speaks to me of the lavishness of the Divine. Fluid beauty is streaming to the universe, to all who are aware and alert. I think of a life lived in love, achieving fullness, with no fear left.

Lady Wisdom, Tree of Life, Holder and Dispenser of Love, of the riches of True Wisdom, of precious life, help me now to put wings to my heels. Give me the fruit of the Tree of Life.

GRATITUDE

Abundance
  is so much more
   than a balance:
    enough to pay the bills,
    and a bit to better
     diminishing dreams of others.

   Long life
    is little
     if lived in loneliness
      latched tightly against loss,
      or keeping armed guard
      with a prisoned soul.

    Enough?
     Yet more
     and more again.
      Each day the blessings
      flood over me,
      a baptism,
       a lavish love
       poured out.

       My thankful heart
       opens.

5

The First Made, Hovering

God created me before the beginning of all,
before all else that was made, long ago.
Alone, I was fashioned in times long past,
at the beginning, long before earth itself.
When there was yet no ocean, I was born,
no springs brimming with water.
Before the mountains were settled in their place,
long before the hills I was born,
when as yet God had made neither land nor lake
nor first clod of earth.
When God set the heavens in their place I was there,
when God girdled the ocean with the horizon,
when God fixed the canopy of clouds overhead
and set the springs of ocean firm in their place,
when God prescribed its limits for the sea,
and knit together earth's foundations,
I was by God's side,
a master artisan
delighting God day after day,
ever at play in God's presence
delighting to be
with the daughters and sons of humankind.

—PROVERBS 8:22–31

HOVERING

Thwapping presence, circling blades,
airborne lights, the guns and roaring,

h o v e r i n g ,

urban police insert themselves,
yet another war zone battle.

Not able to trust, rechecking,
correcting, changing, shaming,

h o v e r i n g ,

my teacher becomes the butcher,
I bury my truth, and die again.

A mother bird returns once more,
weary with weeks of worms and waiting,

h o v e r i n g ,

coaxing chicks. They stretch, and fall,
and finally fly, a bird.

Silent presence in our lives,
brooding on our unfilled dreams,

h o v e r i n g ,

you call us forth to reach and soar
and burst into our finest bounty.

Move across my daily sameness,
wake me, find me, hold me.

H o v e r i n g ,

craft my moments into mountains,
help me too, to dream, and fly.

Play and Delight

I was by God's side, a master artisan
delighting God day after day,
ever at play in God's presence,
delighting to be with the daughters and sons of humankind.

Play and delight! My heart lifted and smiled while I was reading these words. Holy Mother Wisdom, teach me to play in your presence. Teach me the trust as well as the awe that will allow me to play while accompanying my God in the work of creation.

Play! And delight! For someone who wishes to know Sophia better and better, this is an important text. Play and delight. What an attitude to bring to God. We delight when we see this attitude in others. Remember Tevye in *Fiddler on the Roof?* His life was not all that happy but he certainly could play with God. Somehow, however, the weight of teaching around the majesty and dignity of God does not encourage us to be aware of this aspect of the Divine.

As I reflect on this I recognize hints of God's playfulness being offered to me by people around me. My friend, I have been in awe of your attitude these last few days. I see you, an accomplished artist, setting out to "learn about collage" in the most open and public way. With all your expertise in your field you are ready to say that you don't know everything and you are ready to learn a new thing from the very beginning. You remind me of my Breema[1] teachers, who say, "Whenever you begin a treatment, approach it as a beginner." This is a wonderful, refreshing, liberating way to be, to approach something new or old. With the curiosity, playfulness, and enthusiasm of a child. There are no inadequacies or fears to hide. What a lesson for me, the frightened one!

At this time in my life I am teetering yet again on the fence of resolution. I know I need to commit yet again to my personal disciplines, and in the familiar pattern I am stepping down the stile on the "right" side. It is not that I have abandoned my spiritual practice, but again I need to refresh, to breathe life, to go ahead.

I am now using practices from my longish life as a Christian and a nun; I am also discovering, with delighted recognition, practices from women around me who are deeply religious and who have recovered practices which profoundly belong to our nature as created beings. I want to throw myself into them wholeheartedly. I really do!

My journey of renewal has so far taken me from head to body, with dramatic results. Then some months ago I felt called to a new stage—from body into heart. I have prayed daily for a long time to be given the gift of a compassionate and discerning heart, and it seemed that that prayer was moving in me. Around that time I re-engaged in my all-consuming daily round of earning a living, and my energy for the journey dropped. Now I begin to feel it move within me again. I feel reconnected with my spiritual guides whose faces I long to know, and with all the holy souls who have preceded me through this life. I feel connected once again to the vision dimly glimpsed to which they call me.

Creation is a painfully slow business! In medieval times the clergy danced down the aisle in a three-steps-forward, one-step-back metaphor of our daily struggle to be created. This is certainly the way it is for me. I guess the image of this dance should help me laugh with Wisdom as I once again settle by the side of the creating God to bring creation into a new stage of being.

As I write, I recall the encultured/embodied belief of the Australian aborigines that creation is renewed minute by minute, and day by day, by the reverent awareness of the people. Seasonally they travel their traditional routes, camping at traditional sites, where the whole path and its features commemorate the primordial activities of the creator beings. In song and dance the people reverence those creator beings who entered features of the landscape they had created, and in so doing the people continue the work of holding the creation in being. When the group moves on they will leave the land truly blessed, and when they return next season, food and resources will be there for them. For the aborigines, as for other tribal people, life and religion were not distinguished one from the other: life was a seamless garment.

So what is the connection of this memory with play and delight in my life? Cultivating simplicity and integrating as many parts of me and my life as I can seems to be a good idea. Relearning now what came naturally as a child: approaching life with open arms, eyes, ears, nose, and heart; being curious, not afraid.

After all, the Love that is creation is a watchful, encouraging, steadfast presence, hovering over our waters of chaos. This hovering is a time of brooding, of love, of hope, a time of joyous play. There is more curiosity and love in Wisdom than judgment and plan. Like the dance of medieval times our lives travel a somewhat experimental path, sometimes forward, sometimes back. Only time will tell us that the backward steps are as crucial to our journey as the forward.

In the image in this chapter I see light and water spilling richly—the elements of life at its deepest level, without which there is no life and no richness. I see depths of profundity. There are balance and serenity in the repeated horizontals, and movement and energy in the liquid, fruitful, generous gushing downwards. I look for play and notice the red top. Right now the image speaks comfort to me; my journey is not of an unbroken evenness. Creation happens at the edge, when things shift. So let me not regret my lapses and restarts. They are an important element of my growth. They are profoundly human. Instead let me laugh the laugh of fond recognition. Let me trust my God so that I may play with her.

Holy Creator Wisdom, may my journey reverence your creation in myself. Hold me in loving embrace, teach me to be curious and hopeful rather than fearful. Surprise me and help me cope with surprises. Exchange my fears for the risk of play.

WAYS I FOOL MYSELF WHEN MAKING ART

One

(in which I imagine myself alone responsible for my creation)

I work as I am supposed to: alone.
    Wrestling materials to my will,
    my ego sets the rhythm,
    my hands perform, clumsy and obtuse.

      First made was your Companion.
        Your friendship formed the world,
        Her playful touch made all that is.
        Blessing and delight fill all creation.

      What whimsy shaped weasels and whales,
        outrageous orchids, mosquitoes and fleas;
        hopping, crawling, soaring shapes,
        and lumped the leftovers into a platypus?

I

(in which I call forth my wisdom)

Remind me, as I reach for flowers,
    or pigment, or warm, sweet skin,
    together we tumble in hot, juicy space.
    Hover by me, so I too can play.

Two

(in which I think I know what I am going to do)

Expectations usually abort.
    Frozen visions lie petrified.
    My ideas wilt, stillborn,
    I only paint dull death masks.

      Did you foresee the gushing needs
         of water, seeking level space?
         Did you make it lust for moon,
         for wind, and tug of orbit?

      Did you plot the fractal's pattern,
         hiding trees in tiny seeds,
         or placing human spirits
         in chance meetings of single cells?

II

(in which I remember what it is I am doing)

What is left is to begin.
    I clear space, and fence in time,
    toss away the maps and plans,
    and jump into an unmarked journey.

6

Wisdom Enters All

Although she is but one, she can do all things,

and while remaining in herself, she renews all things;

in every generation she passes into holy souls

and makes them friends of God and prophets;

for God loves nothing so much

as the person who lives with Wisdom.

—WISDOM 7:27–29

INVITATION

Irresistibly, your arm unfolds,
glimmering within, twirling, pulsing
to dance steps beyond what I know.

Suspicious, I watch, waiting for signs.
Do tricky steel jaws of traps
lie beneath that promise of love?

Come! you beckon. *You, God's friend!*
Shriveling from your fierce glow,
I shiver, take quick inventory. Me?

How can this be? I am but a woman,
encrusted, old, ravaged by life,
no longer open to such enchantment.

I enter, you vow, *and shadows shift.*
I fill your corners, I widen your life.
But I have enough friends already.

These friends worry my abandonment,
they howl their fear, circling me,
lest I forsake their raucous counsel.

Your smile curls around the sky.
You have minyans who love you,
but listen wisely to their words!

Wither, constrict your costly abundance.
Become finished, polished, small.
They whisper hobbling guidance for life!

No! I call you out from them.
Open your joy, your zest, your passion.
Become even more full of yourself.

Breathe in my love. Stretch your edge,
turn toward me, find my light.
See? Your toes already tap the dance.

Relating beyond Aloneness

In this text Wisdom is bringing holy souls into relation with God. My personal need is to balance relating and aloneness so that my relating is deeper and more authentic. Introvert that I am, being alone has mostly been a refuge and a salve for me, and in some important sense it will continue to be. Yet what has arisen for me lately is a questioning of the quality of my aloneness.

My wanting to be alone certainly provides necessary time and space for me to replenish divine energy. But it is also certainly a mode of escapism and a reluctance to engage things outside myself. My important task now is to discover how to live and grow, acknowledging and dealing with both these tendencies in myself.

One valuable tool I have discovered is the Enneagram. This is a personality-typing system which appears to have been concerned with spiritual growth from its inception. It identifies three basic attitudes to life: fear, anger, and inability to identify emotion. The model suggests that each of us is situated in one of the three basic attitudes as a reaction to the conditions we lived with in childhood. Within each of those three divisions are three more, making nine personality types altogether. The model gives these and other tools to help us identify our stance toward life, but, more important, it is a dynamic model. We are encouraged to change and are supported in the endeavor.

I have been aware of my stinginess with my own time for some years and wanted it to be different, without actually doing anything very constructive about it. Study of the Enneagram shed some light by instructing me that the chief vice of my personality type, the fives, is acquisitiveness. Once I knew this, it did not take me too long to identify my selfishness in the use of my time as my "core" vice. I can be as generous as you like with time, provided I am donating it, but I resent fiercely any intrusion that is not planned. I would again like to alter this state of affairs, for my own health and for the good of those I love and work with.

How to change is the problem, of course. I have tried to uproot undesirable traits and vices and have learned that violence really is not effective in these matters. Slow and steady is a better idea. Also, I need to be aware that eradication of personal traits does not happen—the issues will come up again!

The philosophy of St. Benedict's rule suggests that balance is the key to dealing with life's paradoxes: escaping or defaulting not to either pole, but holding all things in delicate balance. Many times over the years I have heard the words "living with the paradox," and I am struck anew that I do not really hear until a truth impinges on my need. Now, perhaps, it is time for me to grapple with this paradox.

Apropos of aloneness, Benedict teaches that no one may expect to live as a healthy, life-giving, God-loving hermit without specific preparation. This preparation is to experience the abrasion and healing of living in close, demanding relationship with a community of people for an extended period of time. After the shaping and honing provided by these experiences one might then be ready to live as a hermit. The lives of the mystics, too, remind us that we are relational beings. I remember Catherine of Siena's reluctance to give up her exclusive and life-consuming time alone with God. She resented and argued against God's demand that she leave off enjoying God's special presence in contemplation and rejoin her family's daily life, but the demand prevailed.

Speaking from personal experience, I guess that all introverts have been struggling with this issue of being appropriately out there since God first invented the category! My problem is to deal with the downside of my introversion, the tendency to resent life's necessary intrusion on the organization of my time.

The one-to-one lifestyle I now live presents me with a choice and an opportunity—either a fall into inertia through the dread of having my "free" time budgeted by forces outside myself, or a seizing of the opportunity to achieve my greatest desire: to love and be loved by self, by others, and by God.

One of the ways in which I have remained isolated from friends and others has been my adamant refusal to ask for help, feeling that no matter what the circumstances I should soldier on. I am not sure of all my motives in this, but I know that feeling "not worthy" was certainly one of them. There is something for me to learn about this issue from contemporary Australian aborigines. Some years ago I heard a speaker say that the first aim of an aborigine on entering a new community is to put him or herself under obligation to the other members of the group. This is a concept which is probably repugnant to most Western people. Our independence, our ability to do it ourselves, our ability to cope, is a significant mark of our success. However, the ritual serves in part to secure one's place within the new community. How different this is from our stance when entering a new group or toward new neighbors!

Yesterday I said to you, "I am tired and edgy, give me a hug." You, who of course had already noticed, just came and gave me a hug. My being able to say it was a big advance from keeping my difficulties quiet and trying to deal with them myself. May this be the beginning of a new practice for this introvert. It is a gift from and to our careful and loving relationship.

I choose life. And so I must be/do what is necessary. What keeps me connected to my body and the flesh around me? Not willpower. Not self-imposed isolation. I cannot walk the journey alone. This I know by experience and by divine decree, no less!

In the painting in this chapter I see the image of the earth's bones, moving with motion too slow for any human eye to register. Inexorable motion dramatically altering the ground beneath our feet, while we are completely unaware: where living beings once stood on level ground, we now look down into unimaginable depths; where living people once worked and played is now an excavation pit and a place of relics, where fragile human flesh was replaced by fiery stone. I see these bones of the earth, alive with profound power, slow and deep, stretching, growing and straining, working at the long and secret fashioning of this beautiful place where I am called to be. In contemplating the image I feel the power and energy of God impelling me also to live and grow, to become what I can be in God. Yearning arises in me, and a fierce belief. I recognize power at once irresistible and tranquil, working for good and for growth.

Strong Lady Wisdom, your aloneness brought forth life, not desolation and despair. Engaging Lady Wisdom who calls me out of myself, be my strength and guide in living this life of one-to-one relationship to which you have called me—because you did call!

PRAYER

Bone-shifter of the curious,
She who calls forth
my what-if, why-not, how-about;
you squeeze beneath the known,
tickling my sleep,
startling my wonder,
tumbling my comfort,
disturbing the view.

Stir my stillness again today.
My quiet life is too formless.
Greet me running to your table,
an outrageous banquet of delight.
Fill my plate with your bounty:
endless imagination,
churning energy,
sparkling surprise.

You who knew my bones before my birth,
who kept me safe under your heart;
you who groan with the labor
of impregnating me in your image:
do not cast me aside.
Teach me,
baptize me,
name me as your own.

7

Wisdom Searches

Alone I made a circuit across the vault of the heavens,

and returned alone through the abyss of the sea . . .

looking for a home.

—ECCLESIASTICUS 24:5–7

CAKES FOR THE QUEEN OF HEAVEN

Queen of Heaven,
we made these cakes for you,
but where do we send them?

You ride across the heavens each day
and stride across the deeps by night,
alone, searching for your home.

We say you are more beautiful than the sun,
that you illuminate life itself,
placing that spark in every living thing.

We say you are the light of Shabbot.
It is you we welcomed with the sundown,
and rested beside in this sacred time.

How can it be that a queen
who is made of light itself
wanders, and has no forwarding address?

Their dark suspicion hid you.
They abhor your woman power and, shunning,
Scoff at silence they no longer hear.

Homeseeking Lady of Heaven,
teach me to stretch open my own door,
and welcome you home to my heart.[1]

Feeling at Home, Embodied

Wisdom also searches for a home! Until my renewal journey I only knew that I was lonely. Then the focus clarified, and I knew that I needed to find a home. The first step was finding a home in my own heart. Being at home with God was not one step to be mounted and then all would be achieved. I became aware that there were/are many levels of at-homeness I need to achieve in myself, and that this work was the path to being at home in God. As my necessary steps became clear, the first was to become at home in my body. Over time other necessary steps have been revealed.

I came to renewal physically, psychically, and spiritually crippled, and began to work with a therapist, a spiritual director, and later a bodyworker.

My relationship with my body during most of my life was, to say the least, peculiar. As a young person I walked on fences, climbed trees, and played sports with considerable skill. However, along with this obvious ability I also entertained the irreconcilable and irrational belief that I was clumsy and unattractive. Throughout my life I simply treated my body as a necessary vehicle for sustaining my activity. By the time I was fifty years old my neck was frozen, my whole body stiff, and I had been taking prescribed drugs for tension for two years.

After the work with my therapist had begun I had two frightening experiences. Walking along the street one day, I experienced a terrifying feeling of being submerged in water and not being able to breathe or escape. This experience involved all of my body as I felt pressure on my lungs and constraint on my limbs. I stood on the street and tried to remain with the feelings to acknowledge that I was consciously attending to them, but then I had to let them go as something I could not face alone. I did not deal further with this experience or the one below, beyond telling my therapist about it. However, I recognized their significance in the overall theme of helplessness and power with which I was struggling.

The second experience involved a sensation in my abdomen and abdominal organs. I felt as if my abdomen was split open, as if I was coming "unstitched." The feeling associated with both of these experiences was one of helplessness, of being in a situation beyond my capacity to control. These experiences no doubt were related to the hopeless or helpless feeling which then pervaded my life.

As this stage of my journey unfolded, many things said and shown me by my therapist culminated in a birthing experience which helped me deal with my ubiquitous feelings of helplessness. The exercise was simple but was profound in its effect. My therapist advised me to get someone to hold a towel against my head and to push against the towel. The bodyworker did this for me. I lay on the floor full length with my head against a towel held by the bodyworker. As she held the towel firmly to prevent me from pushing through, I felt the old feeling of helplessness flow over me and then, suddenly, I felt a strong resolve to push through, which I did. It was a powerful moment for me and really symbolized a healthy change.

The wonderful gift for me, when I finally began to deal with my inner issues, was that my body, even while holding memories of tension and neglect, became a powerful vehicle of my healing. My bodily sensations alerted me to spiritual and psychic issues to be pursued in my healing task.

What proved most astonishing to me was the connection of my body's health to my spiritual health. I had intellectually subscribed to this truth, but now it hit me with the force of truth possessed in my own body. The healing of my relationship to my body was an integral part of a new, healed attitude to God, to others, and to prayer.

The adventure of coming home to my body has released energy which I never knew was available to me. This energy had its source wonderfully in sexual energy. I have begun to understand the fundamental and energizing connection between sexuality, eroticism, and creativity, dealt with by a number of contemporary spiritual women authors.[2]

Other energies loosened were the stirrings of compassion and the ability to pray differently. In coming to terms with my suffering I came to recognize that all human beings are carrying similar burdens. There is a commonality of human strength and weakness, joy and suffering, a sense of sharing with the rest of humanity in a profound way.

St. Benedict gives no direct teaching on the body. But he does say how the body is to be treated. All the monks are to discipline their bodies because both the heart and the body are instruments of obedience to God's instructions. While this disciplining is happening, the needs of the body are to be respected.

The kitchen workers are to eat early so that they will serve their brothers without grumbling. The sick may take baths whenever it is advisable; they may also eat meat; and they are not expected to keep to prescribed meal times. The reader at meal times will receive some diluted wine because the fast may be too hard for him to bear.

Requirements of discipline are modified for various circumstances. When the monks are to reap the harvest because local help is not available, "all things are to be done

with moderation on account of the faint-hearted." When the work is heavy the abbot may grant some additional food or may alter the times of meals so that the monks will not be faint from hunger.

A choice of dishes is to be offered at every meal. Clothing should be adequate and suited to the climate. During Lent the monk is encouraged to add some personal discipline to that of the regular monastic life. However, the monk must present his penance to the abbot for approval before being allowed to practice it. This no doubt helped to exclude extremes of penance by overenthusiastic monks.

All of this seems to me to suggest that Benedict truly realized the importance of the body. He realized that it is an integral part of our journey to God. He teaches that discipline of the body is necessary and that the body's needs are to be respected. However, he did not seem to recognize the gifts of wisdom stored in the body that I have come to honor and appreciate at this time in my life.

In the painting in this chapter, an orb of light rushes toward me, beautiful rays of light streaming out on either side from it. Above the orb, a heavy curtain of cloud presses from a crimson sky. Below the orb churn waves and rocks, watery rhythms tumbling and pouring across the space. The light from the orb illuminates the space. It is very beautiful and compelling.

Sweet and strong Wisdom, carry me and guide me in my search. Fill me with hope and curiosity. Lead me to my truest home within my body. Help me remember to respect its voice.

HOMELESSNESS

Sour smells announce you. Sidestepping,

    you slither between dark places,

    combing through my cluttered discards, seeking treasures,

    stuffing scraps onto your long-discarded dignity,

    rotting on the bottom of those plastic bags.

    What hope marks your arduous trips

    to territories, street-gossiped, for food or bed?

Or I find you, white hair pillowed on your cane,

    your mouth a cave spring of dribble.

    A house of bulging bags rests, each leaning

    against your sleeping form. Christ-like,

    your half-wrapped swollen feet protrude,

    bloated from exposure and unhealing wounds,

    yet oozing homes for fungus and fleas.

When your hand cries for coins, I shrink,

    not from you, but from the haunt

    of your life-raped story, foreboding clues,

    that Job-like, I too am easily stripped.

    I would need what you know, woman,

    how you survive will be my daily manna.

    How would you receive my cry for help?

Would you return my once-cast spurns with snorts?

    Or are your wounds as Jesus once endured?

    Will you greet me with his compassion,

    long ago shared with friends who too had fled?

    As he did, would you too feed me?

    Bless me, though I once betrayed you?

    Cleanse my fear by comforting my terrors?

How can I turn and pass you by again?

8

Wisdom's Laughter

Wisdom cries aloud in the open air,
she raises her voice in public places;
she calls at the top of the busy street
and proclaims at the open gates of the city:
Simple fools, how long will you be content
with your simplicity?
If only you would respond to my reproof,
I would give you my counsel
and teach you my precepts.
But because you refused to listen when I called,
because no one attended when I stretched out my hand,
because you spurned all my advice
and would have nothing to do with my reproof,
I in my turn will laugh at your doom
and deride you when terror comes upon you,
when terror comes upon you
like a hurricane,
and your doom descends like a whirlwind.

—Proverbs 1:20–27a

NEXT

Your words roar past crossroads.
Wherever even two or three rush past,
who stuff their ears,
who close their souls,
who shun your voice
      and bustle away,
your throat screams out! No sound is heard.

Shadow people hold no space open.
Invisible, like those faceless ones
      whose night dreams come in doorway beds,
      who squat relief between parked cars,
      whose clawlike arms skittle across garbage
      and pull from it their daily breads.
Rushing by their hopeless signs, your cries are smothered.

But others edge from hiding holes.
We've also opened throats with stillborn cries.
      We who bore young ones,
      we the tender, those oozing needs,
      we who labor, earning nothing,
      we who've lived our hair to white,
we cheer you on, Fierce Lady.

We applaud that you turn away.
Laugh, we urge, deep bellied, at their stupidity!
      Bring on the storms, Great One.
      Ride the hurricane!
      Hurry!
      It is time!
We ourselves will stir the whirling winds for You.

Fiery, Passionate, Harsh

In this painting I see an unexpected picture of Wisdom. Such a fearsome painting! The colors meet me first, passionate and harsh. The shapes rise up, angry and sharp verticals; rushing finger-like clouds meet them. The light seems to come from a central source in the top left corner and illuminates the horizon of the landscape below. In the lower right corner, I see hands, applauding, clapping for the holocaust apparently under way.

Anger is not a feeling that women in our (or perhaps any) society have been trained or encouraged to show. Our society and our religion both encourage women to be "womanly," to be of service, to be meek and mild.

I had all the conditioning society and religion can give and on top of that a personality developed by a need to be unseen and unheard. Through most of my life I had an inability to express anger because to express it would have been too dangerous. I needed to keep my head down and not attract unwanted attention. I worked hard to rationalize any anger I felt and prided myself on being able to "let things go." Or so I thought at the time! It became obvious years later that all I had done was push it underground—or better, maybe, under-skin. It was when I stopped to take stock of my life that my anger gushed forth and I was shaken by the knowledge of how angry I really was. In a journal of the time I speak of being surprised by rage.

My rage was all encompassing. I was angry at life and my apparent helplessness and powerlessness over the years; angry at God; angry at the circumstances of life in which I found myself. When the anger first broke, I raged, cried, fell to the floor and thumped it with both fists.

As time went by, specific objects for my anger identified themselves. I was angry with my mother, which was not a surprise. I had suffered for many years from her paranoia and irrational rages, and had spent my adult life trying to stay as far away from her as possible. It was only after letting the anger out that I was able to see that my mother had her own set of problems and frustrations.

What did surprise me was the anger I felt toward my father. He was a gentle man whom I loved and who always loved me, but my anger was directed toward two things. One was that he, the adult, had never protected me from my mother's irrational outbursts. Rather, he would always escape by going downstairs to his workshop, leaving me exposed to her rage. He never thought to take me with him.

Another source of anger arose from an incident that happened toward the end of his life when my mother was hospitalized for an operation. Every Christmas of my adult life when I came home for the holidays my father would ensure that we had some time alone (a difficult thing to arrange under the circumstances) in order to tell me how difficult the previous year had been for him because of my mother. At the time of the operation I had driven him to the hospital to see my mother, and as we entered the hospital he told me that he could only remember the good times when they were first married. I could not allow for his shifting feelings at the time and felt totally used and betrayed as he ignored our shared history. At the time I didn't react, but later!

I was in therapy at the time this was happening, and my therapist suggested practical ways to cope with the rage. Her advice to me was to exercise when the rage fell on me, and this I did. Sometimes I walked furiously and at other times swung a pillow viciously at a large, solid armchair. If no one was around, I made lots of vocal noise. This was immensely satisfying and I heartily recommend it!

During this time anger cropped up all over the place, in all kinds of situations. It would seem that expressing one's anger is a good place to start promoting healing. Certainly it was for me. It was only after expressing the rage that I could forgive myself, my mother, and my father and get past the roadblocks of resentment and even hatred.

Early in this renewal time I was receiving a massage. As the masseuse began to work on the front of my thigh, I pointed out a sore spot to her. She worked on it further and I began to cry and rage. This rage was very generalized, having no particular focus. My body had apparently stored these feelings that my mind had refused to integrate. Her touch released them for me for another opportunity to work them through to acceptance.

It was on another occasion, after a session with a bodyworker, that I realized her aim had been to prompt me to express anger. After getting me to move freely around the room, she began to tease me by flicking at me with a towel. I tried to catch the towel but she evaded my attempts and continued to tease me. I of course became angry and eventually grabbed the towel, ripped it end to end, and flung part of it from a window to the street below. My first great physical demonstration of anger!

The bodyworker continued to engage me in physical exercise. When I became too tired to continue I leaned against a table and began mopping my face with the fragment of torn towel. The bodyworker said to me, "Do you see what you are doing with the towel?" I paused to consider, and said, "Yes. I'm making friends with it, friends with myself."

After much of this kind of work, I had an opportunity to express anger and was able to do so appropriately and without feelings of discomfort. I was a member of a group spiritual direction team and I was able to convey my anger with what I perceived to be poor listening, fragmentation of approach, and lack of development of the group over some months. I was able to sustain the anger appropriately as one member of the group offered inappropriate consolation. I was also careful to offer each person with whom I had interacted an opportunity to process the interaction. Feedback from the group facilitator endorsed my opinion that the anger was appropriate and helpful to the group agenda. It was a good feeling.

I was fortunate when dealing with this issue to have the help of women in therapy, spiritual direction, and bodywork, who were skilled at human development. Under their expert guidance I was able to trust and behave in ways that I had not done before. Also, as I deliberately offered myself up to the work, the realm of blessing opened to me.

In the rule of St. Benedict, anger is mentioned only in that action prompted by anger is considered destructive for the community. We are told not to act in anger or nurse a grudge, not to love quarreling, and if we have a dispute with someone to make peace with him or her before the sun goes down. Perhaps the teaching on humility is the rule's best advice regarding anger and other human capacities and feelings. The ability to see ourselves clearly in the scheme of things is a good way to handle anger. Now I rarely need to express anger and I am confident that it is not building within me like a time bomb. We must grow and change into the image of God, and that process needs constant, faithful attention. There is a need for me to confront myself daily, to bring my awareness to the clarifying light of prayer.

No emotion by itself is salvific, but equally, any powerful emotion if ignored will be extremely destructive of the human personality and spirit. This is true of anger. We cannot ignore it and pretend that all is sweetness and light if it is not. We, especially women, need to be aware of our anger, to examine it and learn how to express it appropriately.

The Wisdom passage at the beginning of this chapter offers a model of when it is appropriate to express anger. In this case Wisdom chastises those who are willfully ignorant, those who refuse to listen. We are called to listen with what St. Bernard called the "ear of our heart," to discern what is spiritually good for us and for our world. And beyond that discerning, we are called to vigorous response. The knowing is not enough. Sometimes we are called to live and suffer to bring about real change. Sometimes we are called to make a hard decision and live with the consequences. Perhaps we are called to leave an abusive relationship, or perhaps we are called to live a simpler lifestyle. Answering these calls takes courage.

Strong and awesome Wisdom, who scorns the willfully deaf, give me strength to remain alert and true; give me strength of conviction and powerful trust in myself. Help me voice your anger and outrage to effect transformation in my world.

TEACHER

Outstretched, her hand compresses the wind.
This time there is no mercy.
Compassion is nowhere in her voice.

I too know this place
where I cry out
and no ears choose to hear.

Invisible one,
such shunning stirs my slumbering ghosts
to lash against such faceless silence.

Turn the other cheek?
You mock such meekness
and spit on those deaf hearts.

Lady Love, I praise your rage.
I take courage in your spurn,
and I sing you to your full wrath.

Warrior woman, show me
the path to my own boundary,
and fill me with such strength to my edge.

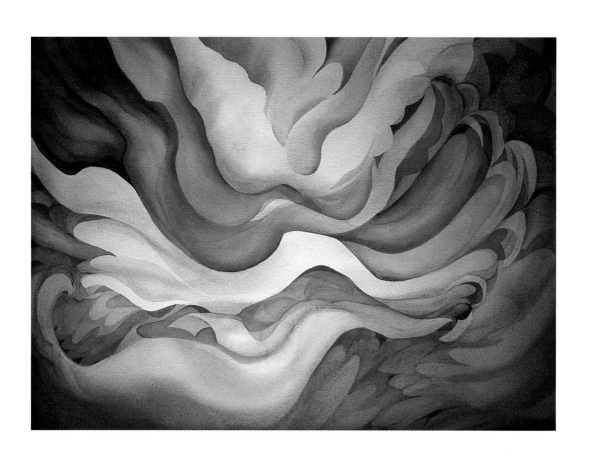

9

Wisdom's Wings

The world considers you a merciful mother.

Bring with you calm and peace

and spread your wings over our sinful times.

—EARLY LITURGICAL PRAYER,
QUOTED IN ELIZABETH A. JOHNSON,
SHE WHO IS

MOTHER LOVE

What Once Was
The landmarks are confused,
fogging memories. Yet I know
the one before you taught you well.
Her hand prints all the patterns.
Rage-raised welts on private places
slash of leather, bruising blows,
yet stoop before the stings of shame,
that strangles spirit with tongue and eye.

Clip her wings! She must not soar.
How I ache for you!
Clitorectomy carves at many places.
Was love so hard a labor?

And Is
Three times I knew your movements deep within.
Crouched low, you grew and stretched
your mark-like scars across my life.
We knitted knowledge of each other's bones.
You form me now as once I shaped your ways.
Laboring long, we tussle power between us.
Who is mother? Who is child?
We moved apart for decades.
Yet each time we speak or smile or kiss
my heart leaps to watch us grow.
Who is teacher? Where the school?
You ripped me open birthing once,
you tear another piece to shape your freedom.

Yet each time you mark me in this strange way
we wrestle not as enemies, but as warriors,
sparring to prove each other's skills.
I wear these birthmarks proudly, battle stars
for wars we both have won.

And Ever Shall Be
Birthing Mother, so wet and warm,
large, looming source of life,
billow bounty, gather 'round
your rustling nest of calm and peace.
Stretch out your womb-wings, bring me home.
Surround me, whirring air,
soft eider quilts of living down,
to comfort, soothe, and rest my soul.
May I pause within your silence?

Caress me. I'll fly once more.
And when I rise to do my work,
glide still below me, ever watchful
to hold me, if I fall.

Dream the Visions

Bless Sophia,
dream the visions,
share the Wisdom
dwelling deep within.

—DAVID HAAS, PRAYER OF THE RE-IMAGINING COMMUNITY, MINNEAPOLIS

As we invoked Sophia thus a few moments ago I felt yet again a profound settling inside myself.

We have sat down to write, but what I really want to do this morning is just be with Sophia, revel in the sweetness of knowing God in terms that resonate in my bones. However, there has to be some discipline! So help me now Sophia. I am here to consider the text and the painting. Let me consider "sinful times."

When I was growing up, sin was something one could do a lot of without really trying, and was definitely something that one had to worry about. The Redemptorist missionaries booming of sin and punishment from the pulpit during the annual parish mission week were very convincing. Sin was a very present and frightening reality. There was mortal sin and venial sin and formulas for telling the difference. Eating meat on Friday, swallowing your tooth-cleaning water before receiving communion, not going to Mass—all of these and more could land you in hell. I beat my breast conscientiously while chanting "Through my fault, through my fault, through my most grievous fault" during the Mass. I worked hard thinking up lists for confession: "Bless me, Father, for I have sinned."

I never felt quite secure about being free from sin, so I aimed for a guarantee. Remember indulgences? If one attended Mass for nine first Fridays of consecutive months, one received a perpetual indulgence as a reward. The same was true of the first five Saturdays in honor of Our Lady. If one completed the required number of services, one could never go to hell. What a deal! I tried valiantly to make those first Fridays but I am not sure I ever completed them. At the time it was very scary and very important, but now, of course, it doesn't matter.

Later in my life came another horror experienced by too many Catholics, the problem of things that could not be told to a priest, could not be told to anyone.

"Scruples" followed—the fear of damnation for making a "bad confession" by unknowingly not confessing all or not confessing correctly. I endured the terror for some years, but eventually came out of it, still unable to tell anyone of my "sin." The evil in this situation was that I could not trust that I would receive acceptance and wise counsel about life's difficulties from anyone I might tell.

I am now in a very different place with regard to the meaning of sin. God forbid (as God does) that I would deny anyone the loving, wise counsel that I could not seek. Also, I have come to realize that an aware journey is the essence of our spirituality, and that this journey has no shortcuts, even if they are offered as indulgences. We tread a spiral path, revisiting traits and tendencies, dealing with the same material at different levels, remaining faithful through times of clear sight and times of no sight and maintaining faith in the constant love of our mothering God. Our journey is cheapened and our faith is made small if we look for shortcuts. Such a view of sin and its antidote is too limited. We are in this for the long haul.

So how do I think about sin now? Social sin is certainly alive and well in our world. Each day the morning paper presents examples of slave labor, immigration scams, poverty, and many other evils arising from our social and economic ethos. I read about and experience the enmity, sometimes political, sometimes violent, between people who worship the same God under a different or even the same name.

But personal sin is, in most cases, not so dramatic or obvious. I have struggled at various times with seeing myself as a sinner. At times it was all too easy to believe that I was condemned to hell; the struggle to avoid this seemed insurmountable. As I look back, it seems extraordinary that this happened to someone who genuinely wanted to love and serve God.

Have I failed in my life? Yes. Have I willed evil? I don't believe so. On the whole my sinfulness seems well described in the familiar terms of "I do what I would not do." There has been inertia in my life, which is, no doubt, the product of my genes and my upbringing, but I reject the extreme notion that I/we are evil at the core. The human beings I am familiar with yearn at the core to do our best against what seem to be high odds.

For myself, I believe profoundly in the "sin against the Holy Spirit," which for me has come to mean willful disregard or willful refusal of grace as it is presented to me. This Easter I have a fundamental understanding that I commit this sin against the Holy Spirit if I refuse to accept that I am loved by God.

The failures I experience are failure to remain aware; failure to "be here"; failure to "stay here." This ancient ascetic exercise is widely used not only by New Age adherents; it is basic to every mystical tradition. I know more and more as I grow older that being present is precious: the times when I can be aware—oh, then I feel the presence of sheltering wings. Then physically, psychically, and spiritually I experience energy for prayer, for listening, and for working at the agenda presented to me by Holy Wisdom.

The Benedictine tradition in which I have lived most of my life deals with the cure for sin rather than discussing sin itself. The tradition calls the disciple to observe spiritual practices in daily life rather than theologize about them. Careful attention to the details of living the spiritual life will result in the monk's growth into the love of God. This careful attention, of course, is not a sterile doing for doing's sake. The monk is to attend to the voice of God in the abbot, in prayer, and in his companions. Above all, the monk is to love and serve Christ, and to do that with vigor. The rule does not contain any formal discussion of sin. It does recognize that we human beings are subject to weakness of body and spirit and that we need to discipline ourselves to grow in love. The cure is to be energetic, aware, and patient.

The painting contains paradox. It reflects for me a sense of both softness and strength, of both quietude and purposeful energy. I can indeed rest on these wings and be borne up. I can experience the lavish, unconditional love that surrounds me. I can receive energy and joy, and love to be shared, not just savored. The image also invites me into mystery. There is more to both me and to my universe than I am aware of.

Wisdom, holy Mother who shelters and saves, you call me to be open above all, to hold myself ready to experience a part, and then another part, of the mystery. You promise me your presence and support. I desire this, now and always. Be here with me, stay with me, pray with me.

AIDS

Just weeks ago
      we cheered the New Year's turn;
      10! 9! 8! blew paper horns,
      7! 6! 5! tossed party papers,
      4! 3! 2! caught each other's eye
      and then we sang
      and kissed each other blessings.

How could we then know
      you would leave us soon?
      tennineeight: intensive care,
      sevensixfive: for days and nights you drifted past,
      fourthreetwo: until we finally said, go well,
      and then we grieved
      and prayed each other comfort.

Mercy, mother! We need you so!
      Damn positive, clever terms,
      X>IX>VIII we bury, bury more,
      VII>VI>V fewer, thinner, bitter graveside gatherings,
      IV>III>II relentless slayer of the race!
      and then we rage
      and flail for dead-end cures.

Evil times! A plague that burns
      one by one our brightest and our best.
      Ten. Nine. Eight. Dan. Todd. Norris. Nate.
      Seven. Six. Five. Tony. Manuel. And even Clive.
      Four. Three. Two. Sally, then Sue.
      And only now we glimpse your wings
      and know we know no peace.

10

Wisdom's Feast

Come to me, you who desire me,

    and eat your fill of my fruits.

For the memory of me is sweeter than honey,

and the possession of me sweeter than the honeycomb.

Those who eat of me will hunger for more,

and those who drink of me will thirst for more.

Whoever obeys me will not be put to shame,

and those who work with me will not sin.

—Sirach 24:19–22

INQUIRY

You're having a feast? Oh! What should I wear?
  Is purple lamé with pearls enough,
  more fetching than a simple black dress
  with tight teasing slits to strut my stuff?
  Do I wear a hat, and heels, and vest,
  and bag? Oh! Which bag would be the very best?

Shall I tease my hair to crispened puffs
  And paint my nails, my lips, my cheeks?
  Will my eyes look best lined gold or blue?
  And wait! My lashes must be tweaked!
  I'll bathe and mask and spray my skin
  with scents and oils that say "I'm in!"

If that's not enough, I'll paint my house,
  I'd weed the yard, then vacuum stairs.
  Perhaps I'll clean the closets too,
  you never know who'll snoop in there.
  I'll polish and sort, wash glass and chrome,
  I'd bake and press, and dust my home.

What else could I do?
  I'll worry and fuss, to rise from the rest;
  I'll accomplish so much I'd be tough to pass up.
  Of course, you'd invite only the best.
  Do I have a chance? Possibly me?
  Everyone else is perfect, you see.

A Cornucopia

Wisdom, you are calling us to your feast. How shall I come? Who shall I bring? The painting in this chapter fills me with a longing to come to the center. I remember all your teaching about the nature of a spiral. I find in the spiral a rainbow of color. Yet beneath that central spiral, I find a quieter, sun-like shape, with an egg-shaped pink center. Is this a promise of life? I see around you unfolding shapes of all colors, unfolding the way my understanding of you has progressed. Then I return to the center and travel again through the outside. Back and forth my eye travels, the entire painting a feast for my eyes, and a promise of the long-yearned-for fulfilled.

The feast is an image of spiritual things important in many cultures. It represents beneficence, plenty, arrival, completion, celebration.

Christmas was the annual feast at my childhood house. A tree was trimmed, and colored paper streamers were strung around the living room. In the midsummer heat and humidity of subtropical Brisbane, Australia, my mother cooked for many hours to produce an immense and somewhat British meal. A leg of ham was cooked in an opened kerosene tin on a fire downstairs. In the kitchen a chicken was roasted and vegetables were prepared: potatoes, beans, peas, and pumpkin. Rich plum pudding and brandy sauce were the next course, and the table held dishes of nuts, dried fruits, and chocolates. Soft drinks and beer were served and in later years a bottle of wine was cautiously added. All this was topped off with hot tea. It was expected, in the sultry climate in which we lived, that everyone would collapse into sleep after dinner.

Later, in my pre-Vatican II novitiate days, the rigor of the novitiate was the result of both the ascetic view of religious life at that time and a lack of funding. Flowing from this, novices were expected to eat what was put in front of them and "feast" had a somewhat different meaning. Some of the feasts concerned consumption of surplus. So, when a new calf was born, we celebrated the extra milk with special milk-based coffee drinks. A particularly unappreciated annual feast was the prolific squash crop. After many days of squash breakfasts, lunches, and dinners, soups, main courses, and desserts, we donned rubber boots and transported the rotting remains to their rest with a wheelbarrow. Laundry day each week (a day of hard labor) was celebrated by a change from bread and spread for morning tea to a mild treat. One famous day we arrived at morning tea to eat the very flat, very soggy cake which a novice cook had made from plain flour when the recipe called for self-rising. On another famous occasion, we waited (in silence) an unusually long time for our boiled sausage Saturday dinner. When the mistress of novices went to inquire, she found that the (again) novice cook had transferred them from a small pot to a very large one containing vast amounts of water because, as she said, "They told me to cover them with water but they kept floating." Needless to say, the sausages were still cold.

We did celebrate individuals' birthdays and religious feast days. These events had little in common regarding menus, though they usually included a celebratory cake. What they did have in common was careful choice of the dishes to be prepared and extra care in preparing the food, the surroundings, and the atmosphere. Subsequent to Vatican II, care was taken by most communities to use the occasions such as birthdays, anniversaries, and feasts as a tool to build community.

The central work of these feasts is food preparation, often the work of women. The event focuses on a meal, though there may be additional ritual connected with the particular feast, including prayer, particular celebrations, perhaps gift exchanges or the honoring of a person or event. Such a feast is often a completion, a celebration of a particular accomplishment.

What often makes a feast difficult for many is the expectation built into the event. There are unwritten, almost unspoken, cultural codes that dictate exact ways to prepare the feasts, and to participate in them. We receive these instructions through family tradition or social mores. But most of all, we hear from our peers about how the celebrations they have attended did or did not measure up to their own expectations. What could be a lovely occasion, however, is often stressful and exhausting. What seems even more bizarre is our desire to measure up to some external concept of perfection as we prepare these feasts.

One topic on which St. Benedict offers no wisdom is the feast. For him food is necessary and should never be an indulgence. He does direct that two dishes should be available at table so that a monk who cannot eat one dish can eat the other. The monks are to receive a pound of bread a day and may receive extra if the labor is hard. Food is certainly an important part of hospitality. A meal is to be offered to guests of the monastery who will dine with the abbot so that the regular life of the monastery will not be disturbed.

If Benedict does not recognize the feast as an important part of life, his teaching on humility does offer wise advice as to the attitude we should bring to the banquet.

A few weeks ago I was reading a section from Benedict's rule that I have read many times before. This time, however, I saw the words with greater clarity. This was a little bit odd because the theme has been of crucial importance to me for some time. I can only say that gifts are given to us at appropriate times. Now that I have really seen these words, though, I am impelled to tease them out for my benefit. The words are these:

> Now, therefore, after ascending all these steps of humility, the monk will quickly arrive at that *perfect love of God which casts out fear.* Through this love, all that he once performed with dread, he will now begin to observe without effort, as though naturally, from habit, no longer out of fear of hell, but out of love for Christ, good habit and delight in virtue. All this the Lord will by the Holy Spirit graciously manifest in his workman now cleansed of vices and sin.

The hook for me, as I have said, is the attractive possibility of deliverance from fear as the driving force in my life, to "arrive at that perfect love of God which casts out fear." Fear has been the underlying attitude of my life: fear of authority, fear of others' expertise, fear of my own incompetence, and so on and on.

For many years I prayed to be delivered from fear but came to realize that something was needed besides prayer. As I entered my renewal journey, one necessary element was quickly revealed to me. I had lived very much as a "head" person. Now I was confronted with the absolute necessity of acknowledging my long-ignored body and its wisdom. I was privileged to do my renewal in a supportive atmosphere and to work with talented and loving women. With their help I came to see that my body was an essential and extremely effective tool in my journey toward integration.

My body-consciousness began on the day the therapist observed that I was clutching part of my anatomy while I was speaking with her. I was oblivious to the fact until she nodded to my hand and said, "What is going on there?" After this the therapist would suggest that the bodyworker begin at a specific place on my body or work with a particular sensation. After many gifts, I was eventually given the precious one of physically experiencing coming home to myself in my own heart. This gift was precious, for with it I understood at last that I need to be at home in myself before I can find home elsewhere and that I could drop deeply cherished regrets concerning my childhood home. Toward the end of my process, when I was struggling to know how to discern a life decision, the therapist said to me, "Trust your body." I now have confidence that my body, if I attend to it respectfully, will guide me in wisdom. Now if fear or anxiety attacks me, I have a place to go and a remedy to use—my groundedness.

During this time I visited a chiropractor, as my ignored and sometimes despised body was in dreadful shape. My spine was out of alignment and I could turn my head only slightly without extreme pain. As the treatments progressed, I became aware that the system being used had more to offer than just aligning my body. I enrolled in classes and now daily practice Breema bodywork, which I can carry over into all the day's activities, keeping me centered and grounded throughout the day.

This confidence in my body has been a wonderful tool in reducing my anxiety, but the job of conquering fear is not done. I need only to take the next step that is offered to me, and my current inspiration suggests that this is a deeper understanding of humility.

I read St. Benedict and think I need to interpret him through women's eyes. Is humility different for women? Over many centuries women have been well taught that they are second-class citizens, subject to governance by men, weaker and more sentimental than men; more (according to the early Christian church fathers) sensual than men (of course, we don't mind that label!) but therefore, of course, temptresses and the root of most evil. There is an extraordinary paradox in the teaching of the Catholic church: on the one hand we learn that original sin is bad and is the fault of Eve the temptress, who inveigles Adam into eating the fruit. On the other hand, however, in the liturgy of the Easter Vigil the words "O happy fault, O happy sin of Adam" are sung with utmost solemnity in a great hymn of celebration. It is obvious that if there is any good to be found in the Fall, it is ascribed to the less proactive Adam. Eve, who actually did something, definitely got it wrong. In some countries women have been awarded only a short time ago the right to vote, own property, and assume financial responsibilities, in other words, to become legal entities. In other countries and cultures these rights for women are not yet a reality. A conservative American church group has recently issued a statement on the value of marriage requiring wives to be obedient to and reliant upon their husbands, based on the words of Paul, and a Catholic bishop has just congratulated them on that move. Statements such as "I am insignificant and ignorant, no better than a beast before you" (Psalm 72:22), and "I am truly a worm, not a man, scorned by men and despised by the people" (Psalm 21:7), which turn up in Benedict and other Christian ascetic teachings, are ones women could apply to themselves without much trouble. I know I could. I had the idea that almost anyone at all was smarter, more authentically authoritative, more talented, more anything else you can think of, than I was.

During my early years as a nun, I tried diligently to comply with all the ascetic practices required in religious life which were supposed to lead to humility. I kept my eyes down, walked quietly, kept silent, guarded my senses in general. But I did not become truly humble. I was so tied up in fear that these practices did not point me in the right direction. My first task was to come to love and understand myself: to realize that I was the beloved of God, that there was a real person here, that I was not some unfortunate accident in the big scheme of things. Telling me I was a worm was definitely overkill. True humility, I believe, can only be known after we have come into our personhood, after we have learned to exercise our authority, when we are at peace with ourselves.

Chapter 7 of the rule of St. Benedict teaches the journey to humility. Much of what he says concerns monastic practices, but there is plenty for all of us to think about. I understand him to be saying that we must live with certain attitudes to God and certain motivations for our life.

The end is to arrive at a place where we are not afraid to surrender ourselves to God, knowing truly, not just saying it, that God is good. We no longer need to cling to masks and personas because we know (wonderful surprise) that God loves the core of us. We can relax in God because we know that our unaided efforts will not get us very far.

How shall I get to this place? Looking at Benedict's chapter 7 globally I see I am called to a number of things: I am required to cultivate an awareness of God accompanying me through life; I need to let God be in my life, affecting my decisions and my actions; I need to listen carefully to the will of God for me; I need to love and trust in difficult times as in good; I need to be candid and open, offering apology where appropriate; I need to be free to let go of burdens and personas which will hinder my journey.

At a recent solstice prayer with some members of my former community, images of me as a child rose up. I saw that I still can act like a grasping, acquisitive child. I prayed for the gift of loving my frightened, grasping child back into the generous child who freely made a decision to give away her doll many years ago to a child who had none. Perhaps this is my direction for this time, to recover the generous child who is free to part with things. It certainly seems to fit. Enneagram fives, as well as being fearful, or perhaps because of it, are acquisitive after all.

Wisdom/Sophia, you invite us to your feast. Let us share in your generative, lavish, loving invitation. Let us come in simplicity of spirit, open and ready to participate. May we truly join with all your creation in celebration at this time. Nourish the fibers of our bodies and spirits. Let us come to the feast of love.

INVITATION

Gather 'round!
Come, heed my call.
I made you each,
I love you all.

Sister spider, bring all who spin,
we need a bridge of your fine silks,
strong enough to join these clans
who, far too long, have lived apart,
assuming each the center of my world.

I need a web, and not these rifts!
Come, spinning ones, and bring your gifts.

Mother Magpie, call your kin
who warble daybreak, sing of sleep.
You fill my silent world with songs,
with chorus, beauty, and with charm
of rainbow colors, in heavenward flight.

We can all soar! You show us how.
Come, flying ones, I need you now.

Luminous leaves, shim'ring in sun,
unfurling from the swell of bud
in dappled patterns of form and hue;
you sheltering space, who dance the breeze,
disguising your wondrous gifts to all,

I thank you, every leaf, for food and seed. And ere
I forget the best: you give us air.

Cats of stealth, ferocious bears,
timid mice and quiet deer,
instincts map your life and moves,
and as you hunt, or rest, or mate,
you take the gifts you want, no more.

I thank you for the life of flesh,
where desire is truth, knowledge that's blessed.

And you who swim, and float, and drift
past sea plants, caves, and sands,
who creep and crawl, who leap and float,
who dart and streak through wave and lake:
teach us to move with grace and skill.

Without two legs, you range the seas.
Come, lead our dance! Come join us, please!

With buzz and sting, with click and whine,
you creeping, crawling, flying ones
who fill my world beyond all count,
who make a tasty meal for some,
or dine on others, or some of each,

a lesson for my feast you make:
you teach us all of give and take.

Rainbow ones, the colors of earths,
you crowning jewels, my spring of delight!
Strong splended souls, close-knitted clans,
you tribes and proud nations, divided, yet one;
bring everyone here, welcome each life.

What matters though is not listed above.
Please bring your Best Gift: teach us to love.

But it's you, old earth, that I call last.
Your craggy cliffs that outlive time,
wild ocean's edge! Thick muds of flood,
strong winds, and rains! Fierce droughts and chills,
scorched by sun, or endless snows.

You are not tamed, or even owned,
yet freely give us all a home.

Enjoy each other's company.
Drink in my love, until
you know no greed or fear at last.
Come to my feast, and have your fill.

Afterword

One of the unusual aspects of the writing in this book has been our approach to the questions of discernment and authority. Without the usual approach to this subject matter, imbedded in scholarship and supported by tradition, we are left with a very subjective base of understanding. To leave this methodology unsupported seems unfinished. So we raise one more complex issue: how do we know what we know?

We recognize that our cultural voices are often our models of learning. From these voices, we seek external authorities who impart their knowledge to our presumably blank and inexperienced minds. We are taught early of the authority of our parents, and then the authorities of our school and neighborhood. It is essential that we have this security. Imagine trying to grow up without access to the gifts of this rich array of knowledge! Yet some of us remain in this way of knowing all our lives. We all return to it constantly, whether it is to get our cars repaired, our recipes consulted, our checkbooks balanced, or our children's illnesses diagnosed and treated.

For some people, this rational, ordered way of managing life works all the time. It is their nature to never question these authorities, to overlook the exceptions, and to expunge the complexities. For others of us, the observations that we make loom too large. What makes some folks get fat, and others remain lean, when intake and exercise remain constant? Why do healthy people sometimes die young? Why do bad things happen to righteous people? Why don't all hardworking people get rich? What makes one marriage last and another fail? Why are innocent children abused? The questions could fill this book.

The conflict comes when we assume that the external voices are God-like. It is true that sometimes God speaks through others, through the church, the Bible, the Torah, the

Qur'an, or other traditions. But we believe that we must always be on guard with these voices. We recognize that even this truth is filtered through the experience of another person, with their life interpretations, their values, and usually their gender. We must find the courage and trust our own wisdom to examine such knowledge, figuring out with our unique point of view whose truth we are viewing, and who wins and who loses in this particular view.

For those of us who have loud internal questioning going on, the picture of God has never been large enough. We need new ways to think, new possibilities, new ways to imagine. Like the plants in our gardens, which occasionally create an unusual flower or stalk (in gardening, this phenomenon is called a "sport," and it is one of the sources of mutation and genetic evolution), some of us are seeing new visions. Perhaps you are one of these.

Like Mary, mother of Jesus, we take in this questioning, these possibilities, and ponder them in our heart. We chew over them in our own lectio divina. We dream. We recognize the authority of this knowledge, and some of us seek to share it with others. We create communities where our ideas are shared, and we can hear the truths and responses of others. We learn also through relationships.

An early dream set a direction for my life.

In my dream, I had died, and was going into a transfer point. There an old man/angel, with stooped back and snowy hair, opened a large book, asking me, "Who were you?" I responded, giving my name. To this, he replied, looking intensely over the top of his glasses at me, "No, no. Who were you?" Startled, I answered that I didn't really know. "What a pity," he continued. "You are the only one God made to be you, and if you never understood who you were, then whoever would?" With this he turned away, slamming the book shut. I woke up sobbing, and never forgot the call of the dream.

It is our hope as authors that what we have given you is a gift of the call into yourself, into your own capacity to know God. It is by telling you our stories, and by showing you through image and word a highly personal approach to this hidden presence, Sophia, that we will encourage you to similarly explore your own life in light of these texts.

Our Prayer for Your Journey

Practice forgiveness, especially of yourself when you stumble, when you accept less than you deserve, or when you take more than you need.

Practice compassion. Hear each other's stories. Tell your own.

Practice hope. Observe that the world is always changing, and take part in helping this happen. Know deeply that what you do makes a difference.

Practice peacemaking. Learn how to listen with your heart, and how to keep your own voice present when negotiating.

Practice love. Show up. Take risks to reveal your truth when it matters. Trust that you can do this.

In following these kinds of practices, may you know Sophia's precious wisdom.

Notes

Preface

1. Quotes from the rule of St. Benedict are from RB 1980, The Liturgical Press, Collegeville, Minnesota.

2. Words of St. Bernard on Advent: "Let it [the Word] pass into the innards of your soul, then let it make its way into your feelings and into your behavior. Eat well and your soul will delight in the abundance. Do not forget to eat your bread, lest your heart dry up, but let your soul be filled as with a banquet" (*The Advent Sermons of St. Bernard of Clairvaux,* trans. Michael Casey, Australian Benedictine Studies Series [Belgrave, Australia: 1970]).

3. Ursula K. LeGuin, *The Farthest Shore* (New York: Bantam Books, 1975).

1. Our Biographies

1. All the paintings are 22" x 30" on Arches cp 140 lb and 300 lb paper.

3. Wisdom Rises

1. *Zimzum:* birth contraction; to contract. If creation is perfected, then no room is present for more to be made. So God contracts or shrinks to make room for new creations. Pronounced "tsimtsum."

2. Joan McMillan, *Remembering the Way,* Menlo Park, California. Ceremony in honor of the labyrinth at Chartres, 1989.

5. The First Made, Hovering

1. Breema bodywork is Kurdish in origin. It is a fully clothed, nonsexual bodywork practice which assumes that the body has enough wisdom to heal itself. The practice is based on a number of principles immediately transferable to life and unites body, mind, and spirit. Breema bodywork is taught at the Breema Institute, Oakland, California.

7. Wisdom Searches

1. See Jeremiah 7:16–20 and 44:15–28 as examples of the ongoing devotion to the Queen of Heaven. While that practice was probably more clearly connected to the Canaanite goddess Astarte

or Ishtar, it nonetheless remains evidence that despite the official prohibitions against the goddess, this devotion remained very active in women's spirituality. For a fascinating discussion of this practice, including preparing the bread in the shape of a vulva and much more detail about Sophia in general, see Asphodel Long, *In a Chariot Drawn by Lions* (Freedom, Calif.: The Crossing Press, 1995), especially page 122. In the poem, I am imagining a similar devotion would be possible to Sophia as the Queen of Heaven.

2. See Rita Nakashima Brock, *Journeys by Heart* (New York: Crossroad, 1988), and Carter Heyward, *Our Passion for Justice* (Cleveland, Ohio: The Pilgrim Press, 1984).